DEDICATION

*T*his book is dedicated to Amy Tincher-Durik, who I admire as an editor and cherish as a friend.

ACKNOWLEDGMENTS

Ask and it will be given to you; seek and you will find; knock and the door will be opened to you. For everyone who asks receives; he who seeks finds; and to him who knocks, the door will be opened.

Matthew 7:7

*I*n writing this book, I asked special favors of the artists, friends, and companies listed below. They responded with the generosity of their knowledge, talents, and time, and I wish to extend a very special thank you.

Accent Import-Export, Inc.
Almac Camera (Jay Jones and Don Felton)
Amaco
Beadalon
Duncan Enterprises
Chris Gluck of Wire Art
LeRoy Goertz
Corrine Gurry
Marilyn Hochstatter
Lynne Merchant
Jack O'Brien of Artistic Wire
QuISHI and Keiko
Preston Reuther
Soft Flex
The Shepherdess (of San Diego, CA)
Wire Artist Magazine

Bird Teaching Friends to Fly by Laura Balombini. Photo by Robert Diamonte.

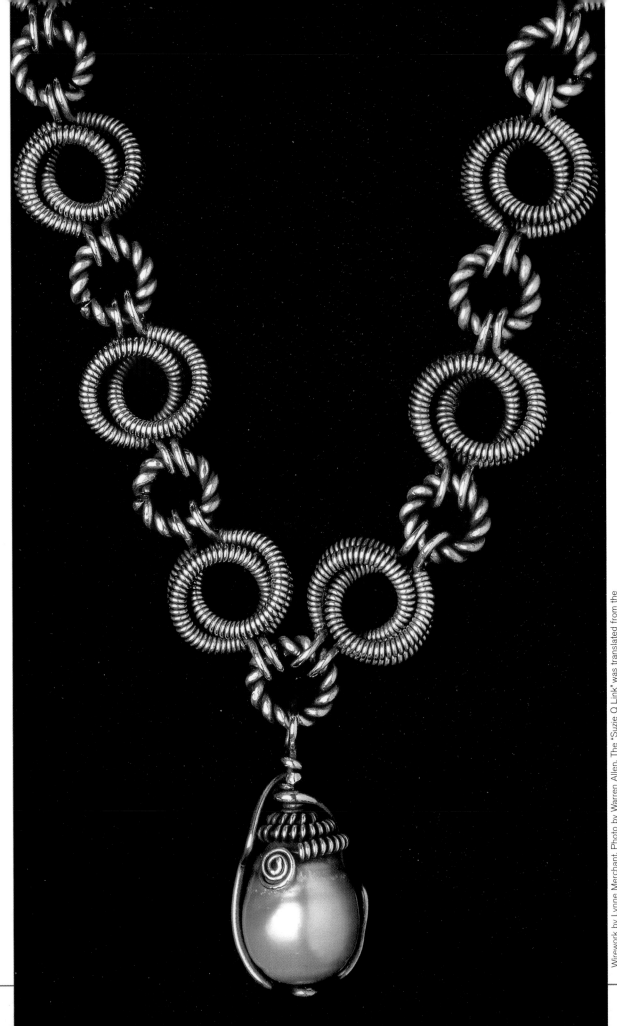

Wire *in* Design

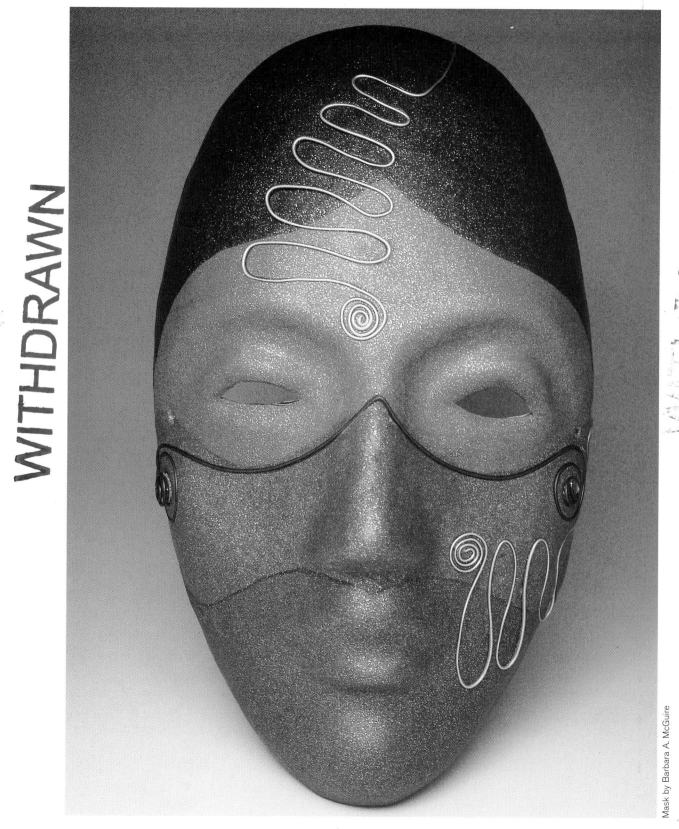

Mask by Barbara A. McGuire

Barbara A. McGuire

Published by
Krause Publications
700 State Street
Iola, Wisconsin 54990-0001
715-445-2214
www.krause.com

Please call or write for our free catalog of publications. Our toll-free number to
place an order or obtain a free catalog is 800-258-0929 or please use our regular
business telephone 715-445-2214 for editorial comment and further information.

Library of Congress Catalog Number 00-111277
ISBN 0-87349-218-8

On the front cover: candleholder by Barbara A. McGuire; earring holder by Celie Fago (Celie
learned the forms used in this piece from New England Tinker Ellen Wieske); earrings by Mike
Buesseler; necklace by LeRoy Goertz (photo by Howard Newcomb).

On the back cover: dog by Tina DeWeese; Celestial banner by Susan McGehee (photo by Andrew
Neuhart); Gaia mobile by Marvin and Michelle Shafer of Q3 Art.

All project "how to" photography by Jay Jones.

TABLE OF CONTENTS

INTRODUCTION

I truly believe there is a wire artist inside each of us that is waiting to spring forth (pun intended). But I didn't always believe that. I thought wire was particular to a chosen few. It seemed so *mundane,* so *plain,* so *common.* Wire is just wire. However, I was wrong in my thinking. Wire is not boring. Wire is not still. Wire is a line, movement, and texture. Wire is alive.

This only happens because people put their soul in it. They put their fun in it. They put their fingers in it. They marry it to their art. Compliment any wire artist, and eight out of ten times he or she will say, "You should see my new stuff!" That statement exemplifies the excitement that is current (another pun intended) today.

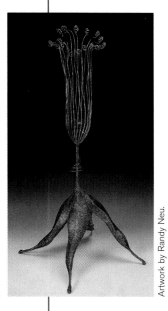

Artwork by Randy Neu.

Wirework is moving forward at a fast pace. It is expanding so much that in just a few months, artists will have developed a new style, a new expression, a new direction. Wire is an everyday acquaintance we take for granted—in telephones, cables, energy, and closets—yet, to the artists on these pages, it is more than a utility, it is a bloodline. It is their chosen medium. It is no longer taken for granted. It is loved. And each strand has a unique personality with an ever-changing character.

I hope to introduce you to a collection of outstanding work in wire and the people who make it happen. Of course, not all wire artists could be included, and there are many extremely talented and creative artists not mentioned or presented. That is not intentional; it is only a circumstance of time and communication. And then there are those yet to be wire artists; it could happen in a second. There are no prerequisites for being a wire artist, and there are no rules as to what kind of a wire artist you may choose to be.

That's why there are so many styles in this book. *Wire in Design* is meant to be pure inspiration. It is a presentation of people from all walks of life and their relationship with art: wire art. Relationships and experience also yield good advice, and that's why there are tips from those who know their stuff. Any beginner can do the projects, but an experienced craftsperson will enhance the design and deliver it with perfection and style. It just takes practice.

Throughout the book, you will meet the artisans who use wire in their creations every day. Insight to their personalities is presented for many reasons: first to acknowledge and credit the work they have presented that inspires and impacts us all, second to glean the advice and information they are willing to share in order for our creativity to flourish, and third to introduce artists as real-life people who are in many ways just like us. Relating to something about a person's character can help us trust that person to guide us in learning. Listening to advice from someone who has worked with a medium for thirty years can prevent us from wasting time and materials. And the privilege of embracing someone's art to go beyond imitation is a gift in its purest form. Many of the artists have been schooled at America's finest universities or have embraced the art from distant shores or exotic places. This should encourage you to learn, to experience the art of diverse cultures, and to continue to seek knowledge about design. The artists have truly given of themselves, and that's what art is all about.

There's another common denominator, one this book couldn't exist without, and that is quality in design. The pieces showcased are attractive or dynamic because they possess value in design. So, at every given opportunity, elements and principles of design are acknowledged and discussed. The projects in Chapter 7 are based on simplistic design, using fundamental techniques, mixed media, innovation, and modern materials. It is helpful to concentrate on simple projects and build as you go. This encourages you, the reader, to further develop your own innovative style. With practice and attention, you will learn to be successful in your craftsmanship and to create a lasting appreciation for wire in design.

Barbara A. McGuire

PART I

WIRE,

PAST

AND

PRESENT

THE STORY OF WIRE

Chapter 1

Wire History: Wire Around the World

Wire goes back to ancient times. Perhaps you have seen an ancient piece of Egyptian jewelry in which the fine linear work resembles wire. Or you may have seen an antique Chinese cloisonné vase and noticed the fine metalwork in the enamel. Wire dates back to biblical times when precious stones were set in gold filigree. Filigree was made by hammering gold or silver into thin sheets and then cutting the metal into thin strips. The strips were filed smooth, making a form of wire.

About 1800-1900 B.C., Egyptian sarcophagus design began to include woven strands of gold and silver, an influence perhaps of the Hebrew artists who had traveled to the land to avoid famine. Often, when ancient peoples traveled from land to land, the migrating artisans influenced the art form of their new environment; however, an art form can nearly or completely die when one culture absorbs into another and preferences are made (for instance, in Roman times, Phoenician wire wrapping may have diminished in favor of traditional silversmithing).

Drawn wire began in France, and during the times of knights and armor, wire was brought back to England to make chainmail. Decorative wire had limited use other than to fasten crucifixes or religious symbols to lanyards and chains. And, in the seventeenth century, Slovakian peasants used thin strands of laminated iron to repair broken pottery.

Eventually, wirework developed into a trade and "tinkers," as they were called, developed their trade into a profession. By the end of the eighteenth century, tinkers had traveled throughout the Hungarian Empire and were making

Chinese cloisonné. Notice the twisted wire in the fruit motif at far left.

everyday objects out of wire. These utensils and tools included animal traps, spoons, ladles, colanders, and baskets. With the migration of the tinkers to Russia, Germany, France, and America, these objects—frames, vases, fruit stands, bowls, and carriers—became more creative and refined.

In 1823, Henry Stammler was awarded recognition for his exceptional wirework at the Exposition of French Industrial Products. This opened the door for a common material to be accepted as a decorative art medium. In the early 1900s, nearly 10,000 tinkers were working throughout Europe and America. Modern techniques in making wire developed, and the most talented flourished in creativity. Baskets and candelabras became quite elaborate, and the work was decorated with tassels and elaborate patterns. Many were commissioned objects that included monograms. As the demand increased, wire objects were offered in catalogs and department stores, and factories were made to produce utensils, baskets, and containers. The most common items, such as rug beaters, corkscrews, whisks, and plate holders, reflected the clever design efforts of their creators. Most of the wire pieces were tinned, but eventually they would rust, and as enamel, stainless steel, and plastic came into the markets, the production of handmade wire objects diminished.

Wire hen reminiscent of French basketry.

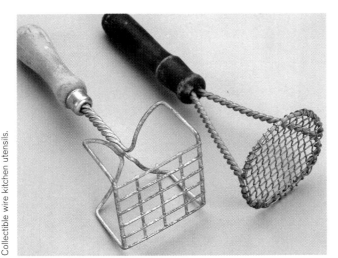

Collectible wire kitchen utensils.

Typical antique wire rug beater in folk art style.

The Story of Wire

Antique French wire designs are again gaining popularity in baskets, hangers, and holders. As charming as the modern renditions are, the original tinkered pieces remain a pleasure to view and seek as a collector's item.

Fashionable wire jewelry appeared in the 1800s when bohemian gypsies used wire to create decorative jewelry. Some of this jewelry included stringing chips of polished glass and stone beads. Aristocrats insisted on the authenticity of the pieces, and copies were jeered at. During the nineteenth century, in a time known as the Victorian age, precious stones in settings were popular forms of jewelry, and cameos were predominant. Wire artists set the stones and cameos and passed their secrets on from generation to generation.

Currently, a captivating form of artistry in stone setting with square wire is emerging which is referred to as Wire Art Sculpture. Techniques are passed on not only through traditional apprenticeship but also through modern means such as video and the Internet. Regardless of the times and the method, technique is being passed on that allows wire artists to create an infinite variety of decorative settings, pendants, bracelets, rings, and artistic adornment.

Earrings and ring-bracelet; modern versions of traditional Peruvian wirework. Photo by Don Felton.

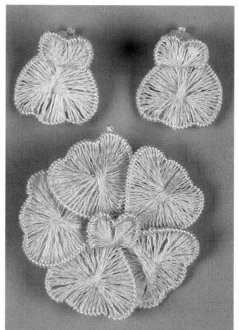

Western German jewelry set.

Antique Moroccan jewelry with glass insets.

Afghani pendant. Photo by Jay Jones.

Tribal art; wire and metal collar. Photo by Jay Jones.

The Story of Wire

Abstract wire candleholder.

Miniature wire furniture, made in China.

Modern gold-painted wire bowl.

Even though there are factories and retail outlets for wire products, all wire pieces, past and present, are essentially made by hand. An artist can gather inspiration from the wire objects that are available in the marketplace. When you see a piece in a store, you can choose to buy it and place it in your home to study and admire, discreetly sketch it in a book for future reference, or scrutinize it and try to reproduce it from memory. The most important aspect in acquiring inspiration from pieces in a commercial setting is that you not compete with or impair the person who is producing the wire object to earn his or her livelihood. Keep in mind this advice from Lynne Merchant: "While you are admiring the work, take the extra time necessary to absorb the essence of the piece and the qualities of the art you find appealing. In that way, when you recall your experience, and allow it to influence your creativity, you will move forward in your work and the most striking elements will appear in your personal interpretation."

■ ■ ■ ■ ■

Information on the history of wire was generously given by Mark Case, Sr., Mark Case Wire Art Jewelry.

How Modern Wire Is Made

I had imagined copper wire was made simply by pouring molten copper into a funnel, cooling it, and winding it on a spool. Not so—and not so easy. The process of manufacturing wire includes many steps that are regulated by sophisticated equipment. The information I received came from Jack O'Brien, CEO of Artistic Wire. His company provides colored copper wire for the craft industry, as well as others, that is used for making such diverse products as fly-fishing lures, hearing aids, and computer components.

Jack says that making wire is like splitting hairs. You can just imagine how precise the manufacturing process is! The process begins with molten metal. Phelps Dodge, who makes copper metal into wire, states that the quality of the product equals the quality of its parts. Copper in its natural, pure state is a soft metal. It can be made stronger by adding other metals to it. The process of combining metals is called antimony. Bronze is an alloy of tin and copper, brass is an alloy of copper and zinc, and sterling silver is an alloy of 92.5 percent silver and copper. All wire is manufactured in the same way; I am using pure copper to describe the process.

Pure copper is manufactured into rods through a process called continuous casting, which includes casting, shaping, and pickling. Casting the molten metal begins by heating the copper in two furnaces, a shaft furnace and a holding furnace. It is important for consistency in the final product that temperatures be regulated and held. After precise regulation, molten metal is moved and shaped on moving steel belts. Eventually, it appears as a 2-1/2" by 5" rectangle. This solid copper rectangle passes through a shaping machine that shaves the edges to make the molten bar into an oval to prevent seams in the rolling process. Then, the copper is passed through a succession of rollers that shape the copper into a rod that is 3/8" in diameter. The rods travel nearly one mile per minute through the machine and are cooled with water. The rods are laid into loose coils. These coils are then passed through a pick-

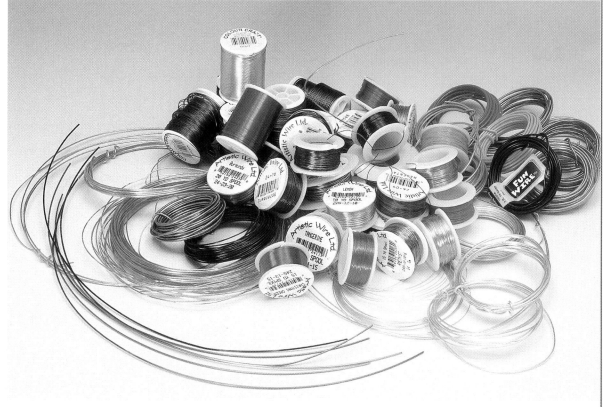

Craft wire.

ling process. The first liquid solution is sulfuric acid that cleans the copper, the second solution neutralizes the acid, and the third solution coats the copper with a sealer that will protect the surface during transport. The wire is laid into a coil—each one weighs 3 tons!

Wire is made smaller by a process called drawing. Pure copper rods are pulled through a series of successively smaller dies. These dies are made of maximum-strength diamond compounds and have exact dimensions and roundness (for example, a 1/2" diameter rod will pass through ten dies to result in 14 gauge wire). As the wire is drawn, it gets hot. It is continually cooled by a water and fat solution called a soap bath. As the wire is being pulled, the friction results in heat, which makes it hard. Now it must be heated again to make it soft and workable; this is called annealing. This crucial step is directly relevant to the ease or difficulty in bending wire. The difference between hardening and softening the wire with heat is the amount of time the wire is subjected to it. The drawn coils are loaded into an annealer, air is replaced with gas and heated to 800° F, and the wire anneals for four hours. Now the wire is soft and can be made hard again by working it (which produces heat), or heating it with a butane torch (which will also change the color). The annealing process is the reason commercial wire is labeled soft, half hard, or hard. Jewelers in particular must purchase a certain softness or hardness to be able to "work" or "design" the wire into a hardness that is supportive.

To make colored wire, the pure copper wire is coated with a series of enamels. Some copper wire must be coated eleven times to achieve the desired results! The enamels are applied as a liquid that began as chemical resins mixed with solvents; they are very special and require precise regulation.

At the same time the enamel is coated on the wire, the bare wire is being annealed. A wiping die removes exactly the correct amount of enamel from the coated wire. The wire is then cured by heat, looped, and the process is repeated. The color that results depends on the dyes in the enameling process. Some colors are only made at certain times of the year because the conditions are so sensitive. A combination of coatings may be required to produce a particular wire; for instance, some wire may have a polyester base coat and a nylon top coat.

Plastic-coated wire is made in a completely different process. The PVC or polyethelene coatings are melted by heat and then forced around the copper wire as it emerges into a water bath to cool and is pulled onto a spool.

Wire may seem like a simple commodity, but, in actuality, it is a tool manufactured with precision.

■ ■ ■ ■ ■ ■

Wire Manufacture at a Glance...

1. Melted and temperature held.

2. Molten metal shaped.

3. Shave bars to oval rods.

4. Rolled rods cooled in water.

5. Pickling process; cleans, neutralizes, and seals to protect surface.

6. Made smaller by drawing through dies.

7. Cooled in soap bath.

8. Annealed.

■ ■ ■ ■ ■

PART II

THE NATURE

OF WIRE

AS A MEDIUM

AND

DESIGN ELEMENT

COSTUME DESIGN BY RENE J. CIGLER. PHOTO BY MONIQUE OZIMKOWSKI. MODEL: CHRISTINA KUTA.

Chapter 2

MATERIALS AND TOOLS

Which Wire Works

The first piece of wire jewelry I ever made fell apart. I had labored over the piece by making special beads and matching them perfectly to pretty pastel wire that was given to me as a gift. The wire was plastic-coated and "looked" thick enough. But I should have realized that it was too easy to bend into those lovely coils. And in all reality, I should not have expected the tiny thread of copper running through the middle of my coils to stay in place. The moral of the story? If it's too easy to bend into place, it probably won't stay there!

After that experience, I started to really pay attention. I immediately got confused and overwhelmed. There didn't seem to be one wire that did it all. Is there really that much difference between gauges? And what do you do with that really thin stuff anyway? To make the different kinds of wire understandable and comparable, I decided to chart my findings, combined with the recommendations of others. That way, when I wanted to make something specific, or I liked something I saw, I could relate to the gauges and make a good estimate of which gauge would be appropriate for my art

piece. The raw metals and materials that wire consists of also have different properties. The quality, strength, and durability are usually reflected in the price. That's why a spool of cheap wire may do for a party centerpiece, but you wouldn't want to make a bracelet out of it. And that's also why you wouldn't want to put copper in your pierced ears; some wires rust and others tarnish.

Colored wire is usually copper wire coated with paint or plastic, but there is also color-coated steel wire, and the performance and quality are not equal to base metals. Aluminum wire can be anodized to produce an awesome range of colors, although it is susceptible to scratches. And new plastic-coated wire is being manufactured in an extremely festive variety of colors. Most plastic-coated wire is PVC (Polyvinyl Chloride), but it also can be polyester. This poly-material may or may not anneal to polymer clay. Some PVC, and even metal wires, may not be appropriate for use because of toxicity issues; for instance, you cannot assume that stainless wire is appropriate for food use. The wire that utensils are made of is produced in extremely controlled environments. For that reason, it is best to know what your materials are before you begin your work.

Wire gauge (shown actual size).

Wire Comparison Chart

Gauge	Metal	Coating	Application	Strength and Flexibility
14-16	Copper	None	Good structure for baskets or sculpture and some jewelry (such as bracelets).	Strong and flexible; holds shape well.
18	Copper	None	Good for light basketry, jewelry, jigging, wire portraits, sculpture, craft projects.	Strong and flexible; once bent, it is hard to completely straighten kinks. Needs to be hardened to hold shape.
20	Copper	None	Embellishment in crafts, wrapping found objects, ear wires, wrapping coils for beads.	Average strength; easily wrapped but needs to be hardened to hold shape.
22-24	Copper	None	Embellishment in crafts, wrapping stones, and holding found objects, earrings, wrapping coils for wrapped beads.	Not supportive strength; overworking will snap.
16-18	Copper	Plastic	Craft sculpture, basketry, jewelry, line art.	Flexible, although kinks may be hard to smooth out.
20-22	Copper	Plastic	Craft sculpture, bunching, wrapping, jewelry, line art, wrapped wires, beads, found objects. Works well with gizmo, great for kids or whimsical pieces.	Very flexible, kinks smooth easily; may weaken or discolor with age. Will hold coils but not freeform shape under strain.
24	Copper	Plastic	Crochet, wrapping, stringing beads for kids.	Very flexible, kinks smooth easily; may weaken or discolor with age.
14	Sterling	None	Core of wrapped beads, heavy jump rings.	Strong, holds shape; reworkable if wire is soft.
16	Sterling	None	Core wrapped beads, wrapping, basketry, heavy jump rings.	Strong, holds shape; wire easily reworked if wire is "soft."
18	Sterling, Soft	None	Wrapped wire, jewelry.	Very flexible, smooths easily; strong.
20	Sterling, Soft	None	Earring wires.	Earring wires should be "half-hard" sterling.

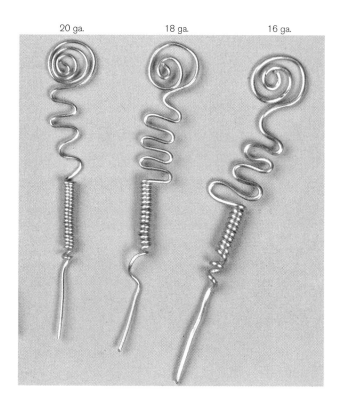

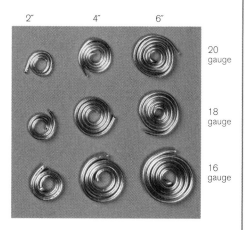

Left and above: Copper wire in various gauges and lengths.

Materials and Tools

Gauge	Metal	Coating	Application	Strength and Flexibility
22-24	Sterling	None	Wrapped wire, jewelry.	Very flexible, smooths easily; strong but must be hardened to hold shape.
18-20, 22	Copper	Paint	Crafts and jewelry, wrapping.	Very flexible, smooths easily; strong but must be hardened to hold shape; overworking will snap wire.
24-28	Copper	Paint	Crochet, knitting, wrapping, stringing, crafts and jewelry.	Very flexible, smooths easily; overworking will snap wire.
18-22	Niobium	Anodized colors	Jewelry, mobiles, sculpture.	Very lightweight; bends easily but may snap. Surface can be nicked, removing color.
18-24	Fine Silver	None	Art jewelry, fine art sculpture.	Soft and flexible; delicate.
18-24	Sterling	Gold-filled	Jewelry, wire wrapping.	Stiff, hard, unpredictable.
18-24	Sterling	Gold-filled; square	Wire sculpture jewelry.	Project dictates hardness.

22 gauge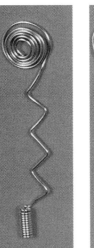

20 gauge

18 gauge

16 gauge

22 gauge 20 gauge 18 gauge 16 gauge

12"

Left and above: Sterling silver wire in various gauges and lengths.

18 gauge gold square

20 gauge silver square

20 gauge gold square

16 gauge niobium anodized

Tools and Their Uses

■ Essential Tools: Reaching for Perfection

When I was a skier, I soon learned that having good equipment helped me go faster. Since that time, I have always believed that using good tools was one of the best things I could do to improve my art. Of course, I have also been stubborn in refusing to accept any advantage other than that with which I was born. I have an appreciation for my hands, and often the raw moment of creation flows regardless of the tools available. Now I have learned to appreciate both the raw and the perfect. The tools presented here will help you accomplish your work. They are not meant to do your work, only to enable you, the artist.

It is suggested that you begin to practice working with copper wire. This will allow you to advance in skill and create samples in a less expensive material than sterling. You can also experiment with gauges and lengths before you actually sit down to make a finished piece.

The basic technique information I present came from an outstanding class instructed by Lynne Merchant, who is featured in Chapter 5. Her methods are what I consider to be essential skills—the correct way to make an eye pin, wrap wire, make a spiral, and to snip, as well as what it means to have a respect for your hands and your tools. With these basics, designing in wire is unlimited. You are encouraged to seek out good instruction and partake in classes that can further develop your skills. You are encouraged to seek mentors who inspire you. And you are encouraged to read and study the elements and principles of design (see page 29). Seeking information can save you a lot of mistakes and money, but the best way to absorb something is to learn by example and then actually experiment in a hands-on setting—and it takes more than one bend, more than one wrap, more than one snip.

In some cases, the instructions and simple ingredients are the most valuable tools, as in this marvelous kit by Chris Gluck, of Wire Art, Duncan Enterprises.

■ Tools Are an Extension of Your Hands

This may be a little uncomfortable at first, especially if you are used to working only with your hands, but you will learn how valuable tools are when you use them correctly and they perform as you desire. It is also important that you learn how your body can help you. Pay attention to the leverage your arm supplies and the pressure you subject your fingers to. Sit or stand in a position that enables you to move freely. Do not wear constricting clothes. Never use your fingernails or teeth to bend wire. In fact, fingernails that are too long get in the way; cut them off! Sit up straight with both feet on the floor and give yourself enough light to work in and enough rest to remain alert. This may seem like common sense, but you'd be surprised at how few people actually do it.

■ Essential Tools

Incredible work can be accomplished with very basic tools. It is wise to invest in the best round nose, chain nose, and flat nose pliers; the price will usually reflect the performance. Compare the quality of tools made in Sweden, Germany, and Pakistan. High quality tools can enable the artist

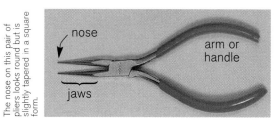

The nose on this pair of pliers looks round but is slightly tapered in a square form.

nose

arm or handle

jaws

to design with ease and precision and prevent nicks in the wire.

A good **work surface** will prevent tools, wire, and beads from moving around. You can use a piece of craft foam or leather, or a synthetic or woven material that will prevent beads from rolling around the surface of your worktable. Dark wide wale corduroy is an excellent choice.

It is not recommended that your pliers have serrated teeth on the inside of the jaws. It may appear that the jaws would grip better, but these tools will mar the wire's surface.

Round nose pliers are essential for making curves in wire. "Round nose" means the jaws of the pliers are completely rounded and taper to a point. These pliers can be either short or long nose and actually work as a mandrel when you are creating a ring.

It is helpful to remove the spring from your tools so that you may employ the full spread of the jaws. Your hands will do less work if they are not resisting a spring.

Flat nose pliers are completely flat on the inside of the jaws and can be angularly tapered on the top and sides of the jaws. The tip is squared off. These pliers are good for making angles in wire. The thin, flat tip also helps to pry between wires that are close together and grab wire firmly. Good flat pliers will not dent the wire as you are working. Sometimes it is necessary to refine the tools with a super-fine file, including the inside surface of the jaws, so the pliers can do their best work.

Chain nose pliers are flat on the inside of the jaws and rounded on the outside of the jaws. They are good for gripping and bending in tight places, as well as holding wire at different angles. They are predominantly used for making the angle on an eye pin. The flat and chain nose pliers are commonly used together in opening and closing eye pins and jump rings.

Flush cutters are used for cutting wire. They should have a flat surface on one side of the blade and an angled surface on the other side. Thus, when a piece of wire is cut into two pieces, the tip of one side of the wire will have a flat cut and the tip of the other side will have an angle cut. You must pay attention so you work with the piece that has the flat cut. You may have to re-cut a piece, just so that the wire has a blunt end.

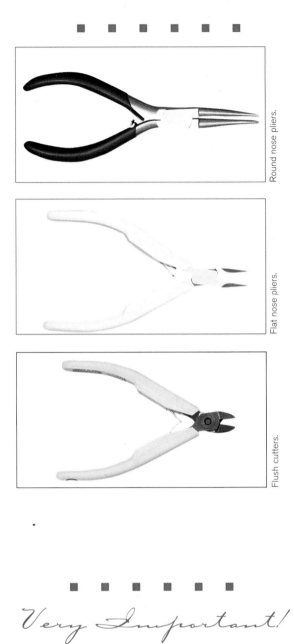

Round nose pliers.

Flat nose pliers.

Flush cutters.

Very Important!

Please refer to the instructions on cutting wire (see page 25). The wire must be controlled and held in place at all times. A piece of flying metal is extremely dangerous. It can go anywhere—into your eye, disc drive, electrical socket, or food, not to mention your child. It is not only your body that must be protected from flying metal. This is an essential habit to develop!

A **mandrel** is used as a form to wrap something around. It is good to have a collection of several pieces of wood or metal in different sizes to use as mandrels. The jaw of round nose pliers is often used as a mandrel when bending wire.

Files are used to sand away snags and points in wire. Needle files are inexpensive and are used for jewelry and wire.

■ Additional Pliers and Specific Uses

Teflon jaw pliers enable an artist to hold a piece in place without scratching the wire. The jaws must be replaced from time to time.

Needle nose bent pliers have long jaws that bend in an angle and allow the artist to grasp the work from behind. This helps the artist see the work from an unobstructed view.

Jump ring pliers have jaws that are sectioned into different diameters. The top jaw has a curve that conforms to the shape of the lower jaw.

■ Tools That Will Flatten or Strengthen Wire

A **metal hammer head** is used to flatten and change the shape and surface of the metal in a wire strand.

A **Teflon or plastic hammer head** is used to harden wire without changing the shape.

An **anvil** is a block of metal used as a surface for pounding wire or metal.

■ Finishing Treatments to Enhance Wire's Beauty

Liver of sulfur is a chemical (read label warnings for toxicity) that will oxidize or tarnish metal. It comes in a solid form, usually little rocks, and must be purchased from a jewelry supply source. It should be kept in a dark, dry location. (See page 28 for usage instructions.)

Steel wool (0000) is used to polish silver after it has been dipped in a liver of sulfur solution.

A **polishing cloth** intensifies shine and removes traces of tarnish.

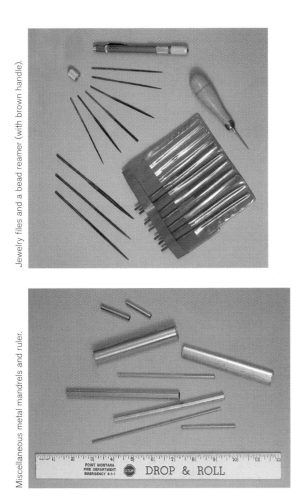

Jewelry files and a bead reamer (with brown handle).

Miscellaneous metal mandrels and ruler.

DROP & ROLL

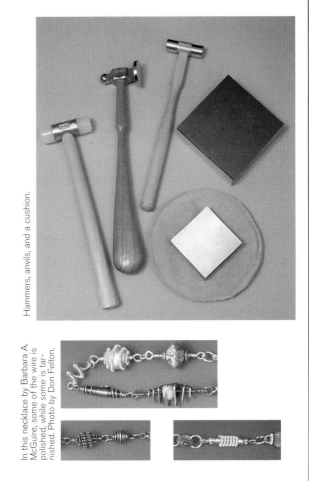

Hammers, anvils, and a cushion.

In this necklace by Barbara A. McGuire, some of the wire is polished, while some is tarnished. Photo by Don Felton.

Special Tools and Jigs

These tools were designed by individuals to make wireworking easy or consistent. You can accomplish similar results by hand or by using homemade versions of the tools, but in our modern world, we seek to save time, add convenience, and avoid strain (if you use your hands incorrectly). The look of a tooled piece is somewhat different from the look of a hand-worked piece; machine tooling will create more exacting results, while a hand-worked piece will reflect the touch of the artist.

■ Hardening and Flattening Tools

There are many special tools designed by people who have experience in working with wire; one such tool is called the **Whack-It-Down**. This tool consists of two pieces of loved-toughened acrylic. A wire shape is placed on the acrylic slab, and it is hit or "whacked" with the other acrylic slab. The momentum of the blow stiffens the wire, making it harder and less flexible.

■ Jigs

You have probably seen a piece of metal or acrylic with numerous little holes and pegs used as a **jig** for bending wire. This is a rendition of the old-fashion tool made from a piece of wood with nails. The modern tools offer flexibility in changing the pegs easily. Each version of this type of tool has its unique advantage. The pegs can be arranged to **loop or shape the wire** in specific patterns. This is very useful when you are trying to repeat the exact same pattern. It is also useful when you are experimenting with a new shape or creating long lengths of a looped pattern.

Wig Jig and Spiral Maker.

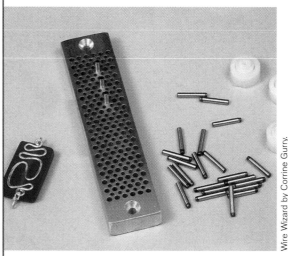

Wire Wizard by Corrine Gurry.

There are also tools available that will make **wrapping wire** very easy. These tools allow you to spool the wire around an interchangeable rod or mandrel while you turn a handle or crank. Some are held by hand, and some are braced on a table. More sophisticated versions, such as the Deluxe Coiling Gizmo, secure the core wire with a chuck and rotate the core as the wire twists. This type of tool can create very long pieces of wrapped wire. Traditional wire wrapping by hand wraps one piece of wire while the mandrel (or wire core) is held stationary.

Twist 'n' Curl, a hand-held twisting tool by Donna's Designs.

The Coiling Gizmo by LeRoy Goertz. Inset: Project by LeRoy on page 80.

Work Hardening

It is very important how a person chooses to work with wire because of something called work hardening. This means that the wire is worked into a stiffer metal as the artist constructs the piece. You can hammer it, twist it, bend it, and pull it through a duct. As wire bends, its molecules change, which stiffens the metal; however, if the wire is stiffened to such a degree that it can no longer bend, it will remain either stationary or snap under pressure. Each metal has its own characteristics, but no matter what metal it is, the degree to which it has been hardened in the manufacturing process is relevant to what you can do with it. Each metal has its own ductility (ability to be drawn through a plate) and malleability (its ability to be molded into shape). Sterling silver, in dead soft hardness, is extremely user-friendly, brass (copper, tin, and zinc) is rigid, copper is flexible but cannot be re-straightened easily, and gold is usually gold-filled and has the personality of whatever metal is underneath it (the base metal). This is also the reason that an artist needs to practice and physically feel the stiffening result of bending the wire. Only by handling the wire will you understand its tolerance, strength, and flexibility.

■   ■   ■   ■   ■

Fundamental Instructions

When learning any craft, it is much to your advantage to acquire solid, basic techniques on which to expand your knowledge and skill. I had tried to accomplish these skills independently, but the results were not consistent, and the wire was often damaged. Artist Lynne Merchant taught the following presentation of techniques to me. I consider these methods to be the correct way to approach wirework. It is to her credit that this instruction is made available. It must also be noted that dead soft sterling wire will produce optimum results for the techniques presented, and other wires may have unique characteristics that will produce different results.

■ Preparing Tools

It may be necessary to file any corrosion or debris from your tools so they can perform to the best of their ability (Figure 1). You may notice that certain tools need refinement because the workmanship is not always at its optimum. Some people may also wish to remove the spring from tools, because this will widen their potential grip, as well as allow them to move freely.

Pliers are gripped with one arm of the pliers held by the thumb, and the other arm of the pli-ers woven between the forefinger, middle finger (pointing to the palm), and ring and pinky finger (on top of the arm of the pliers) (Figure 2). This allows your tools to be an extension of your hands and enables the mobility of the forefinger.

■ Measuring

There are two reasons to measure consistently and frequently. One is so you are aware of the materials you need and do not waste them. Another reason is that when you wish to make identical pieces, you can measure to achieve the same size of piece or midpoint. Often, while working, you can measure the amount you need to finish a piece with a ring or spiral to know when to stop a wrap (Figure 3).

■ Straightening

To straighten wire, there are two options. One is to run it over the edge of a table, exerting pressure where the wire meets the table, which helps to remove kinks. Another method is to stroke the wire between the thumb and forefinger, holding the fingers spread apart, with the thumb being vertically higher than the forefinger (or vice versa) so the wire is straightened between two pressure points that counter-balance each other. The wire will follow the direction in which the top finger is pointing.

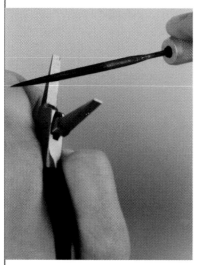

Figure 1

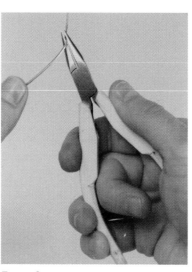

Figure 2

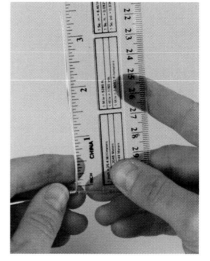

Figure 3

Cutting: Extremely Important!

When a piece of wire is severed, the cutting tool exerts pressure, and the pieces are propelled apart with an extreme force that is dangerous to humans and objects. The wire will fly if it is not restrained. You must spread your fingers to hold both stems of the wire on either side of the cut as it is made (in other words, you must hold both the piece you wish to keep and the piece that is being cut off) (Figure 4). This is an important habit to acquire in working with wire.

In the instance of snipping a tiny piece or end, hold your finger over the end piece so the tiny particle can be stopped by the finger and guided to a trash receptacle (Figure 5). When you are working in wire, most pieces should have a blunt end, so you may often need to re-snip an end before you continue to work.

Filing

File sharp edges and points with a tiny metal file made exclusively for jewelry or fine work. File in a consistent direction, pointing away from your body. File tools with a flat jewelers file to remove corrosion and to resurface the jaws. The holes of beads can also be routed with a special file called a bead reamer file. This will enlarge the opening to accommodate a larger gauge wire.

Looping the End to Make an Eye Hook

To make an eye hook, two pliers are used, a long round nose and a chain nose. The wire length is measured to accommodate the loop and flush cut to have a blunt end. The wire end is placed in the jaw of the round nose pliers just at the point where the pliers grip the metal. If you touch the jaw with your finger, you should not be able to feel the wire poking through (Figure 6). If the wire pokes through, the resulting shape will be a

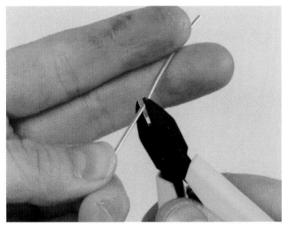

Figure 4

Figure 5

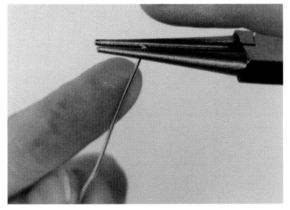

Figure 6

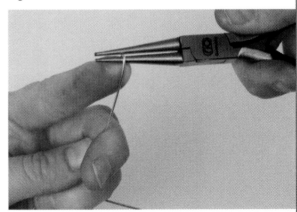

Figure 7

teardrop as opposed to round. The wire must be gripped tightly to ensure the metal will not slip. This is the standard way to begin a turn.

Working at the top of the pliers' nose produces a smaller circle than working at the back of the jaws (near the box joint). The wire is gripped, the pliers are turned away from the body, and the wire is bent around the pliers, which serve as the mandrel (Figure 7). The pliers are released and repositioned to grab the wire in the same place on the jaw. Continue rotating the pliers and bending the loop to form a circle (Figure 8). Use the thumb on your opposite hand to guide the wire around the mandrel-jaw (Figure 9). The circle is formed, the pliers are switched, and the chain nose pliers are now inserted into the eye at the position next to the closure. The wire is held firmly while the chain nose pliers bend the eye backwards at an extreme angle, away from the closure (Figure 10). The pliers are again switched, and the round nose pliers are reinserted to the full circle, and the wire is gripped while the circle eye is bent forward into an upright position

(Figure 11). The circle should be positioned directly on top of the straight wire. If the circle does not come to a complete close, it can be corrected by holding the side of the eye with a pair of chain nose pliers and working the eye back and forth until the eye is tightly closed (Figure 12). Do not squeeze the circle into place; this would put pressure on the eye in an exact point that would stress the metal. Squeezing the eye together also risks ruining the circle shape.

■ Jump Rings

Jump rings are small circular loops that link elements of jewelry together; they are also used to make a chain. Jump rings can be made by wrapping wire around a mandrel in a full circle to create a coil (Figure 13). Cut the coil apart one ring at a time. Make sure the cut is flush on both sides (you will need to re-cut one of the ends every time to make it flush). Hold each side of the ring with a pair of pliers. It is important that you use pliers with flat inside jaws because

Figure 8

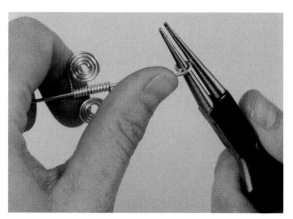

Figure 9

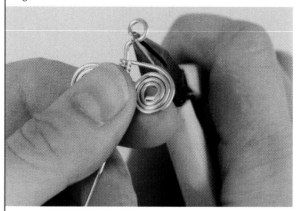

Figure 10

Figure 11

this will not dent the rings. You don't have to purchase two flat pliers because both chain and flat nose pliers are flat on the inside (while round nose pliers will dent wire while you are gripping it). Grip and work the eye halves back and forth to come together (Figure 14). This is how all jump rings should be opened and closed.

■ Wrapping

Wire can be effectively bent and wound over a cylindrical (or oval or square) form called a mandrel. Mandrels can be any diameter and made out of a variety of materials. Often, wire itself serves as a mandrel and as the core to a wound piece, which will later be used in the creation of the design.

The measured length of wire is bent in half and placed over the mandrel to assure proper leverage. A few wraps secure the position, and the wire is held stationary by one hand, while the other hand does the wrapping. The work is slid to the end of the mandrel so the winding movement does not interfere with the mandrel. The wrapped wire is then gently bent about 6" from the mandrel to form a type of crank or handle. One hand holds the wire with the mandrel stationary, and the free hand winds the wire over and around the mandrel with a consistent motion that employs the entire arm. The wire handle is held loosely, and the fingers allow the wire end to spin with the movement to prevent twisting and torquing of the metal. When the wire is wound to the point where the crank is too close to grip, the bend in the wire handle is straightened, the mandrel is slid to another workable position, and

another handle is temporarily fabricated. The work continues until the measured length is wound on one side, then the piece is flipped. A few coils are unwound to regain consistency, and the winding is resumed as described above to finish the entire length. The entire process takes about three minutes to produce a 6" wrap.

■ Hammering

There are three important things to take into account when hammering: the metal, the hammer, and the anvil. The anvil is the bed on which the wire lies while it is being pounded. This dense metal piece should rest on a cushion to absorb the momentum of the blow and deaden the sound.

The softer the metal, the easier it will be to hammer. There are two reasons to hammer the wire; one is to change its shape and texture, and the other is to strengthen it by work hardening. There are two basic types of hammers: metal head hammers and non-marring head hammers, made of materials such as plastic or rawhide. Plastic hammers will not dent or texturize wire but will work-harden the form, adding strength. A steel hammer will dent or flatten the metal itself. The actual shape of the hammer's head will also aid in the intended use of the hammer. If the edge of the hammer is constructed with an abrupt angle, an angle or dent will appear in the piece being pounded. A rounded edge on the hammer will eliminate linear shifts in the pounded metal. The hammer should be held comfortably at the end of the shaft so the leverage of the swing delivers the full force of the blow.

Figure 12

Figure 13

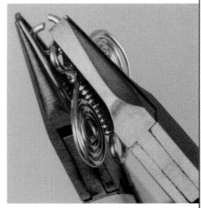

Figure 14

To make a spiral, the wire end is gripped as all turns begin (see eye hooks). In making a spiral, you generally start at the tip to create a small inner circle. The inner circle of the spiral is smaller or larger depending on where you initially grip the wire, near the tip or toward the back of the pliers; this decision affects the size of the resulting spiral. The pliers are turned away from the body, and the wire is bent around the pliers, which serve as the mandrel. Complete the turn as if you were making an eye. Once the inner circle is formed, the pliers are returned to the original position, and the next ring in the spiral turns up and on top of the original circle. The original circle becomes the mandrel. Now you have to switch pliers because you need to hold the spiral as you add layers (Figure 15). Chain nose pliers are best because you can grip the spiral toward the back of the pliers, creating the leverage needed to stabilize the spiral; they serve as an excellent vice. The thumb of your opposite hand will continue to create the spiral. The thumb pushes the wire away from you as the wire coils around itself. It should not push the spiral out of the tool, but should be held at a slight distance for optimum leverage. Whenever you exert pressure away from, instead of toward, yourself, you have a complete range of motion. The leverage is then correct. The spiral is continually repositioned in the back of the pliers so the leverage allows the wire to wrap around itself to form the rings of the spiral in a circular bend without angles (Figure 16).

Air will naturally tarnish silver, copper, and brass because air has sulfur and additional compounds in it that react with the metals (the patina is a thin film of corrosion that forms on the metals as a result of oxidation). Liver of sulfur (potassium sulfide) is used to chemically darken metal (see page 21; read the label and contact the manufacturer for information on toxicity). This instantly adds age and distinction to a piece. Polishing also influences the resulting look.

Dry chunks of chemical (a pea size) are mixed with about a cup of extremely hot water and dissolved; this hot water raises the temperature of the metal, allowing it to take the patina quicker. The piece is completely submerged for a few moments until it is tarnished. It is taken from the sulfur bath and thoroughly rinsed in clear water. It is dried completely and buffed with 0000 fine steel wool. The piece is again washed with soapy water to remove all traces of steel wool. It is then polished with a silver polishing cloth. This cloth works best because it leaves some oxidation on the piece, in the hard-to-get places, giving it depth and character. You can wash jewelry at any given time to renew the luster.

Tarnishing, buffing, and polishing metal will give it age and distinction.

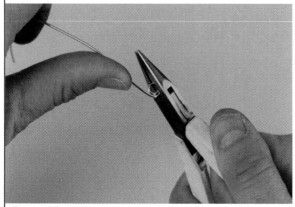

Figure 15

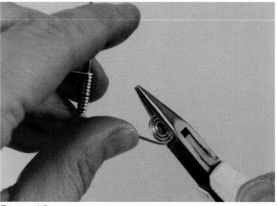

Figure 16

ELEMENTS AND PRINCIPLES OF DESIGN

For anyone who hasn't had a formal art education, there is a topic of study well worth pursuing. That is the basic concept underlying the elements and principles of design. Information on art concepts is frequently found in graphic design books. This is because the organization of the presentation is critical to communication; however, the concepts apply to all media and all art, as well as architecture, fashion, and interior design. In the early twentieth century, the Bauhaus school of design stressed the fundamental concepts of elements and principles, as well as the three "C"s, creativity, craftsmanship, and composition. Through later years, a lot of fundamental teaching was lost to technique rather than design theory. Modern techniques and materials are attractive, but nothing can substitute for quality design.

When you study art elements and principles, you will find that they are not always referred to by the same exact terms. What the various authors are

Flower Lariat by Shana Astrachan. Photo by Chris McCaw.

trying to say is that regardless of what you call them, there are basic concepts, and they express and organize communication in art. Consequently, it is advantageous to utilize the power of proven concepts in the artistic expression of purpose and beauty.

The following explanation of elements and principles is minimal and directed toward using wire. It is a reflection of my personal research, schooling, observation, and experience. It is meant to guide the reader, not to dictate a rule. The introduction to each project in Chapter 7 describes the elements and principles as they are intended to benefit the composition of the projects.

Elements of design are color, value, shape, form, line, space, and texture. Principles of design are balance, pattern, rhythm, movement, contrast, emphasis, and unity. The elements are the components of the art that have certain characteristics, and the principles describe how these components and characteristics relate to each other. The elements are what a piece of art *is comprised of*, and the principles are the *qualities a piece of art has*, produced by the combination of elements.

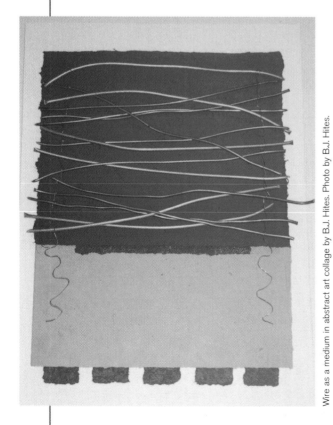

Wire as a medium in abstract art collage by B.J. Hites. Photo by B.J. Hites.

Elements

■ Color

Color is a personal thing; there's no correct way to choose it. Color is an infinite choice. You can even become comfortable with a certain selection of colors and still have infinite variation. But universally, color communicates certain things to us from experiences in the environment in which we live; for example, red stimulates and blue relaxes. These are generalized statements, but colors *can* be used to communicate a mood.

Hue is another word for color. There are basically six hue families: red, orange, yellow, green, blue, and purple. Depending on how much of one or another color is mixed together, the hue will change into a different color. Reds will become orange-ish, and blues will be become turquoise. This is called the undertone. Saturation describes how pure a color is in relation to the basic hue family. If a red has green added to it, it is no longer pure; it is muted or de-saturated. When the red, which is now muted, is combined with blue, it will produce a muddy purple. That's because the red has been muted with green, which has yellow, and dulls the purple. If a color has white added to it, it is no longer pure. Adding white is referred to as tinting the color. Adding black is referred to as shading the color. When a color is muted, it is still identified as one of the six hue families. When a color is de-saturated it is not easily identified; an example of this would be browns or earth tones.

The primary colors are red, yellow, and blue, and the secondary colors are combinations of the primaries that produce green, orange, and purple. In a composition, complementary colors, those opposite each other on the color wheel, will compete for attention, and may even clash. Adding a monotone or a neutral color such as black, white, or gray will separate the competing colors and allow the eye some relief. When choosing a palette, it is common to choose colors close to each other on the wheel, for example, blue and green, and then add a contrast to highlight the combination, such as yellow. Highlighting with color adds attention to that color. Background colors serve as a support to the highlights.

You probably have heard of warm and cool colors. This means that one color, for example a yellow, can look warm or cool and orange-ish or greenish, depending on the other colors mixed in. When creating a palette, it is advisable to mix your colors from the same hue family. If you choose a warm yellow, do not choose a cool yellow to mix your green; there will be something uncomforting about your palette, and it may be hard to recognize. That's because the clashing color is mixed into the green, and it is not related to the other colors. It would be better to mix the green with the warm yellow to make the colors relate.

Everyone wants to know which colors to put together. There is no right answer with wire, because the color is already there, so you may need to develop an eye to distinguish what hues, warm or cool, are in that color. Luckily, silver and black are neutral colors, and brass and copper are de-saturated colors and should go with almost anything. Recognize how you can use this to your advantage in selecting the other elements for your design.

Value

Value is just as important as color; in fact, **it is more effective to vary the amount of value than to vary the amount of color.** Value means the intensity of light and dark. If all of the colors have the same intensity, the piece will look monotonous. Value also adds dimension to a piece. The dark areas will recede, whereas the light areas will move forward. Value can also be associated with mood or feeling. Light generally communicates soft, delicate, spatial, and arid. Dark is by nature associated with heaviness, rich, intense, and enclosed. Grouping light and dark together creates a contrast or impacts sensation and excitement, while grouping pastels or light values together induces tranquility, peacefulness, and calm.

Shape

Shape is an outline or a two-dimensional description of an image or spatial area having depth and width or contour. Often, a shape will abstractly communicate something in reality, such as a leaf or house shape. Shapes can be rigid and straight, or flowing and round. Shapes don't necessarily have to be defined by line; they can be made of color, a block of text, or an area described by texture.

Shapes are the building blocks of images. A drawing of a tree, for example, is the combination of a trunk shape, the shape of the branches, and the individual leaf shapes. Shapes are strong images of communication. We recognize a heart shape, a flower shape, and a hand shape because

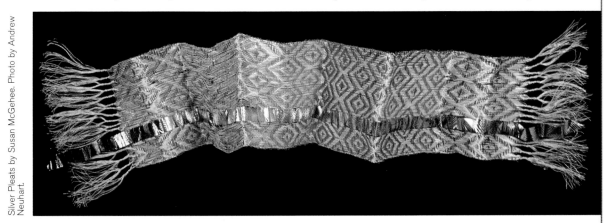

Silver Pleats by Susan McGehee. Photo by Andrew Neuhart.

our mind uses these shapes to represent something in reality. These can all be fashioned in wire to aid in the creation of communication in art.

■ Form

Form is the three-dimensional volume of a piece that has height, width, and depth. A form can be a solid mass or a simulated structure enclosing space. Form follows function. In other words, a candleholder must actually hold a candle, and a basket is built to contain something. While constructing a form, an artist must keep its purpose in mind. Like shapes, forms can be geometric or organic, composed of angles or curves. Forms are as variable as shape or color. A slight variation in a form can produce uniqueness and stimulation and still render the accomplished purpose of the design. A form is often created by enclosing space with a wire structure.

■ Line

Wire is essentially a line. The element of line alone carries the artistic credence of wire. Like wire, lines can be short, fat, curvy, straight, alone, or in a group. The lines have relationships with each other. A line can divide the group, and a single line can lead the eye away from the group.

A spiral is a line of deep historical and primal association. It has been used for centuries to symbolize life and eternity; it is a line that is familiar and beautiful that can be utilized in wire in infinite ways.

■ Space

Space is the powerful understatement in design. When working with wire, space will allow the line and movement of the wire to have their full impact. The more you work with wire, you become comfortable with space and realize that it is not empty but it is actually a component of the design itself. Space is also the phenomenon that brings things closer or farther into view (and therefore perception). If one piece is on top of another, it is closer to the viewer. Space creates a dimension. In creating with wire, we can use the element of space to add depth, form, and balance to our work.

■ Texture

Texture is the tactile surface of a piece. In wire, a simple twist creates a texture, as does a wrap or spiral. Texture is the feeling your fingers experience when you touch your art. Your eye communicates that touch through seeing texture. Texture is a great tool for variation and adding interest in a design. Sometimes wire can create texture in a piece merely because it is raised from the surface of the design.

Turquoise and ivory single necklace by Barbara Becker Simon. Photo by Rob Stegman.

Principles

Balance

Because of gravity, we have an innate understanding of balance. Something must be balanced to keep from falling or leaning to one side. We find comfort in balance. The same is true with wire. The design elements carry a visual weight; busy areas need space to balance the intensity of the detail. Balance can be identical or a mirror image. This is called symmetry—a mirror image is absolute symmetry. If something radiates from the center, it possesses radial symmetry. Asymmetry is when different elements balance each other visually, but do not literally match. A truly balanced piece will put the viewer at peace, while a piece that is intentionally unbalanced will create tension.

Pattern

Pattern is the repetition of line, shape, or textures that organizes to form an overall design. This design can be contained in a single line or a complete surface. The surface patterns can be organized into lines, stacked squares, alternating bricks, or diamonds and often include suborganizations. The key to pattern is repetition. All patterns repeat some of the same elements or motifs, but variety and contrast in shape or color add interest to the pattern. Value also adds depth or dimension to the pattern.

Rhythm

Rhythm is the repetition of visual movement. It is the beat or tempo of the elements' arrangement. When something diminishes in size or value, it creates rhythm that leads the eye. The repetition of something pointing in the same direction will also encourage movement of the eye. Waves upon a shore are not identical to each other but they possess rhythm. In working with wire, the curves or bends create a rhythm when repeated that lead the eye of the viewer throughout the piece.

Movement

Movement is the ability of the elements and principles to lead the eye through a piece of art. Wire is a line, and it moves the eye along the line. It points in a direction, which the eye naturally follows until the line comes to a halt, and another element will grasp movement and continue to lead the viewer. This can be illustrated by a bead on a cord, which leads the eye to the head and back to the bead. In wire, the movement of the eye jumps from one line to another.

Contrast

Contrast is the odd man out. It calls attention to something in particular. It is interesting to contrast textures or colors, because each brings excitement or distinction. You can contrast an element by variation of size, shape, or value and by separating the element from a group. Too much contrast will entice the eye to move back and forth without any purpose. Contrast should be utilized so that it helps to emphasize the focal point of the art and draws attention to the complete work, as well as its individual components.

Emphasis

Every piece has a focus, whether it's communicating an idea or presenting a particular feature of beauty. You can achieve emphasis by quantity and/or quality by placement, such as the middle, by eliminating anything that is distracting to the focus, or by making a single quality stand out in contrast to the other design elements. Emphasis is the core of the design's communication.

Unity

Unity, or harmony, relates to the overall composition and how the elements produce a whole design. Unity is a group of elements that purposefully relate to each other. This means that you can't have the entire art world in every piece. It means that you read one book at a time. In a mystery novel, all of the characters relate to each other; they are all necessary. There are no "extra" characters. It means that everything happening in the piece—the background, the elements, and the theme—belongs to the piece. For example, you wouldn't find pots and pans in the living room (it wouldn't "work"). Once you're willing to let go of everything that does not belong in the composition, your art will have more unity, beauty, and impact.

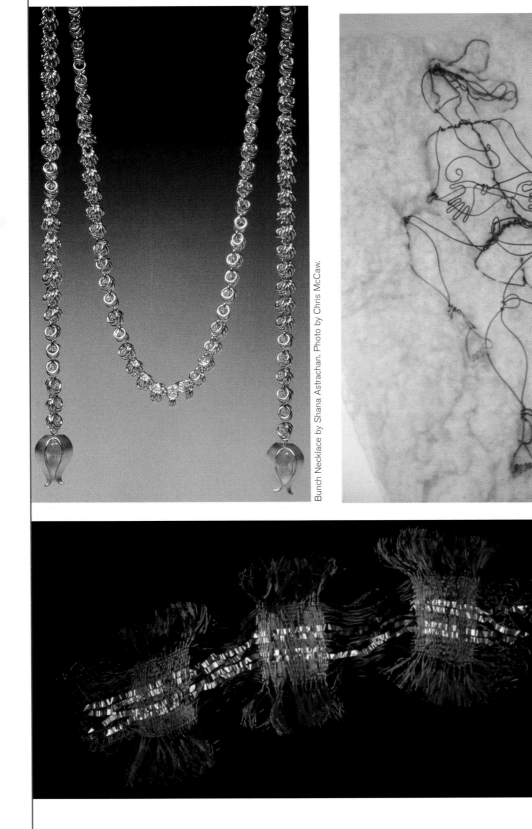

Bunch Necklace by Shana Astrachan. Photo by Chris McCaw.

Cottonwood bed by Tina Deweese.

Liquid Fire Triptych by Susan McGehee. Photo by Andrew Neuhart.

PART III

THE MANY

FACES

AND

PERSONALITIES

OF WIRE

COSTUME DESIGN BY RENE J. CIGLER. PHOTO BY ROGER FATICA. MODEL: ANN SWABB.

Who can conjure up the image of an artist? It could be a picture of anyone you have ever met. Whatever the physical attributes, the images usually include a smile and a studio. Here are a few snapshots for you to enjoy, so you will feel right at home in the company of artists.

Barbara A. McGuire (left) and Lynne Merchant.

Veena Santhigoset.

Timothy Rose.

Kathy Peterson. Photo by Andy Newitt.

Sherie Yazman.

Diane Karg.

Wire As an Art Medium

Chapter 4

WIRE AS AN ART MEDIUM

What is fine art? Is it a concept or a medium? Is a craft less than fine art? These are questions that arise when trying to divide something into categories and groups, and there are no correct answers. And the answers are always changing. In this chapter, I am introducing a group of artists together because their work is conceptual, art for the sake of art. In general, it has no particular utilitarian function. This chapter includes sculpture, mobiles, abstract art, and wall pieces. The artists presented here paint and sculpt with wire. To them, wire speaks because it is perfect for the expression of their creativity. They have dismissed tradition and brought wire into the world of fine art.

Amber Dew Series by Susan Marie Freda. Photo by Almac Camera.

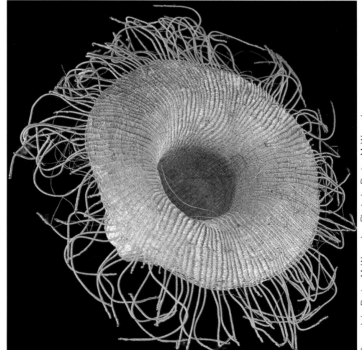

Wirework by Razine M. Wenneker. Photo by Razine M. Wenneker.

Alexander Calder (1898-1976)

If you are going to have a wire artist as a mentor, there are many to choose from, but there is one man whose name is synonymous with wire—and he is the best mentor you can find. Alexander Calder had an impact on the public at large with his ingenious art. He used wire, both functionally and as the entire medium, for a number of pieces. In short, wire was a friend to Calder. He made wire toys and circus figures, he connected wonderful metal shapes with wire in his mobiles, and his drawings even look like they could be drawn with wire. In researching his work, I discovered he produced over 16,000 pieces! The entire art form of mobiles is accredited to his talents. And his art delights millions of viewers nearly every day (there are over 5,000 websites that appear with references to him).

Each of Calder's pieces is delightful. It has been written that this is an extension of his personality. It is encouraging that our delight can find itself into our art. This is true inspiration, that which is innate can be expressed through a visual means, one that transcends time. The freedom and imagination that Calder exhibited serve as leadership for each of us to constantly move forward into an unknown realm, to embrace discovery as it occurs, and to be fearless in our expectations of our art.

Calder loved line, he loved space, and he loved movement. He knew the power of a single line, and he designed with space as an asset. At one time, I had thought of space as being empty; I always had the inclination to fill it. Artists that design with space have a definite advantage, because they use that element as a priceless component to their work. And it is free of charge—in most cases, there are no financial burdens in using space! In the case of Calder, he used real living space as part of his art. And to top it off, the space was constantly changing. His lines create movement, both as an art principle and as a structural reality.

Calder has been an inspiration for many wire artists, including the artists featured on these pages. His wire figures will always serve as a testimony to the artistic potential of wire, and his mobiles will forever place wire as a structural line element.

■   ■   ■   ■   ■

Calder knew the power of a single line, and he designed with space as an asset.

A tribute to the work of Alexander Calder is presented in these postage stamps.

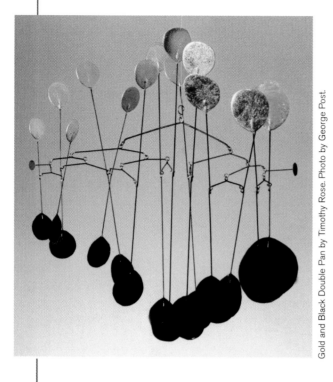

Gold and Black Double Pan by Timothy Rose. Photo by George Post.

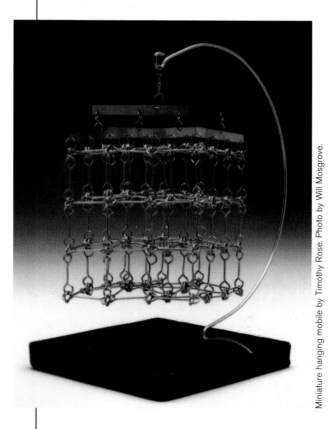

Miniature hanging mobile by Timothy Rose. Photo by Will Mosgrove.

here's a man sitting in a lounge chair on the grass, next to an art booth of spinning color. It's a sunny day in Marin, CA, and Timothy Rose jumps from his chair to enthusiastically explain the dynamics of the mobiles dancing in the gentle breeze.

According to Timothy, mobiles are based on a simple theory: you start from the bottom, not the top (see the following page). In fact, he teaches how to make mobiles to both children and adults and has written booklets, developed kits, and produced videos. Such is his willingness to share in the fun of creating your very own mobile. But looking behind the logical explanation of the physics, you see an artist who has perfected his craft for more than thirty years. Indeed, it would take me thirty years to balance just one of those mobiles, much less imagine the shapes and colors that are united in any of his mesmerizing pieces.

Timothy found his passion from studying the work of Alexander Calder. He explained that Calder would look at his friends' paintings and interpret the composition as sculpture. He introduced movement to sculpture, thus creating the mobile. Calder used many influences from his peers to incorporate into his work, such as Miro's pan shape, Matisse's leaves, and Mondrian's color palettes. Calder's background in engineering served as a reference to the rhythm in his mobiles and the counter-balance of weights that creates the movement.

Timothy begins his mobiles as drawings or paintings, and some paintings can inspire more than one mobile. The actual mobiles are simply 3-D line drawings in space. If you stand underneath and look up into some of the disk-type mobiles, you will see the shapes that are reflected in the original painting. Some mobiles are based on a carousel disk rather than on a bar, such as Calder's mobiles. Timothy's lofty warehouse studio serves as the perfect environment for the creation of sculpture in space. Under one roof, it seems as if the mobiles are alive, talking to each other as they reach across the ceiling.

The essence of the mobile is movement. This is the articulation of one piece causing the movement of another piece, much like the human body—the finger is connected to the wrist, is connected to the elbow, is connected to the shoulder... Early in his experimentation with mobiles, Timothy dismantled clothes hangers and straightened the wire to create mobiles, but a turning point came when he discovered welding supply houses with a vast variety of metals and strengths available for his work. At first, he used found objects, such as seashells, but later he cut shapes from metal or wood. Some works remain in the natural material but most are vividly painted in stripes and simulated texture.

Timothy's work reflects his life as an optimist and someone who is always active. For many years he studied figure drawing, never seeing the same thing twice. Now he strives to capture that essence of change in the mobile. Even in the morning or the evening, you behold a different work of art.

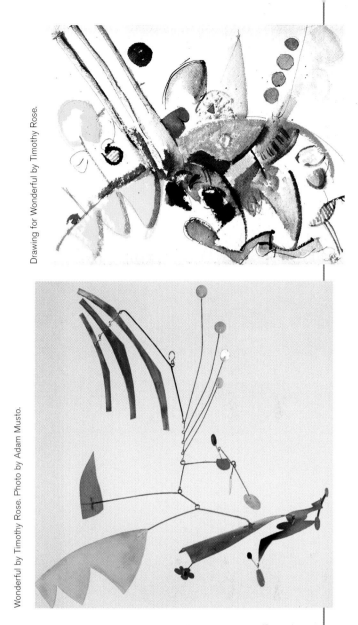

Drawing for Wonderful by Timothy Rose.

Wonderful by Timothy Rose. Photo by Adam Musto.

■　■　■　■　■　■

The Secret: Start from the Bottom and Work to the Top

There are many ways to design a work of hanging sculpture, and as many materials, but the assembly is always the same: start from the bottom.

1. Find and create the shapes you wish. Select and arrange the pieces. Lay them on a large piece of paper. Draw lines connecting the bottom or end pieces.

2. Begin wiring the pieces. Start with the small end pieces, then connect the middle-size systems together.

3. Connect the top. The top bar is last. Connect the middle systems to the top bar, balance, and hang up your new creation.

For more information, see www.mobilesculpture.com, Tim's website.

■　■　■　■　■

Tina DeWeese

Red mobile by Tina DeWeese. Photo by Tina DeWeese.

How does she do it? That's the only thing I could say when I gasped at the wonder of Tina DeWeese's wire. Whoa! These pieces possess so much movement they look as though they are alive. They *are* alive. They have completely captured the energy of a vibrant artist.

I am in awe of the perfection of the art elements and principles. The use of space is extraordinary, and the visual weight balances perfectly with the detail. The shapes and forms are so identifiable that they portray not only an image but also a mood. I can only humbly say that this is what I want my work to aspire to.

Tina has provided an interview, which comes in the form of a statement. Rarely is so much beauty stated in such elegant and simplistic terms. But then again, that is precisely the nature of her art:

"It is an intimate familiarity with these figures which draws me to contemplate the subtleties of animation in motion and at rest, and which inspires me to draw them into the multiplicities of posture and poise that delight my eye and accompany my soul in these simple pleasures of daily life, curiously resonant of my own mood, gesture, and posture. The forms that evolve sometimes happened despite my intentions, the figures somehow assuming a life of their own. I've learned to step aside a bit to let them become their own presence."

■ ■ ■

"I've learned to step aside a bit to let [the figures] become their own presence."

--Tina Deweese

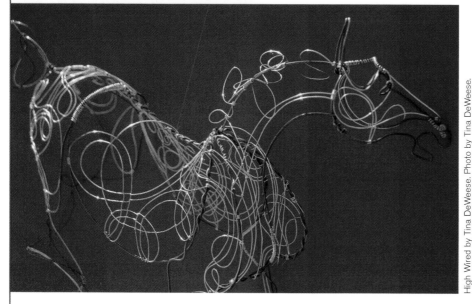

High Wired by Tina DeWeese. Photo by Tina DeWeese.

The concept of a mobile is as variable as art itself. The common denominator is suspension and movement, but the theme, materials, and colors all represent the individual expression.

Steelmobile by Rob Wielgoszinski. Photo by Steve Sparks.

This 'N' That by Marvin and Michelle Shafer of 3Q Art.

Close-up of Steelmobile by Rob Wielgoszinski. Photo by Steve Sparks.

SuMoBile by Marvin and Michelle Shafer of Q3 Art. Photo by David Bentley.

Wire As an Art Medium

Gail Siegel

In her teens, Gail was impressed with her brother, who studied art at Cooper Union. Likewise, she sought the value of art education. Her studies included sessions at universities like UCLA, NYU, and the California College of Arts and Crafts, but she never graduated. She had enough credits, but not the required classes like chemistry and language. And even though the subjects she chose did not focus on wire, you can see the core of educated sophistication in her design.

In her childhood, Gail had access to studios with art supplies. In the early '50s, when she was 8 years old, she received a kit with colored wire to make little figurines. Gail fell in love with wire, and her mother had to keep re-ordering the wire to encourage Gail's creativity.

Eventually, Gail moved onto other interests. Many years later she began dating an artist, who stimulated her interest in art. She gravitated to craft and wire. Gail used any type of wire she could find, including hardware store supplies and building mesh. Gail says she has more wire in her house than she can ever use, but still she is always looking for new materials.

Gail begins her sculpture with no consideration of functionality. She only wants to emphasize form and the medium. Gail has a particular

Red Tray by Gail Siegel. Photo by Carson Smith.

fondness for bowls and vessels. "Bowls are so all-inclusive, they hold, the form is inviting, it has no barriers. There is something warm about the form. Something that draws you inward to the essence of the piece."

With one glance, you can see that Gail's work is really well-constructed and perfected. Her friends consider her to be extremely detailed, neat, and precise: "I like things to look both classy and amusing. The form is familiar, the execution is meticulous, and the combination of materials is unexpected." Gail explains that designs are classy when things are in order. Life is messy, but there is something appealing in order. Grids, fencing, and mesh all have a comforting order to the composition. The texture and repetition also come from our innate sense of order. The pieces are nice to handle, nice to touch—it's like putting your hand over waves.

Some of Gail's pieces take eighty to one hundred hours to make. Gail allows her creativity to be therapeutic and often works on her pieces at night. She often has several pieces to choose from at any given time, including knitted work. She will prep a piece and pick up another to continue stitching, winding, or weaving. Gail often gathers inspiration from fiber shows. She sees something attractive and wonders how it will look in wire. The influence is not a copy but an interpretation. She ponders what would happen if she expanded on that inspiration. As Gail provides inspiration for others to ponder, the circle is continuous.

■　　■　　■　　■　　■　　■

"I like things to look both classy and amusing. The form is familiar, the execution is meticulous, and the combination of materials is unexpected."　　　　--Gail Siegel

Alphabet Soup by Gail Siegel. Photo by Carson Smith.

Boing Boing Chess Set by Laura Balombini. Photo by Jeff Baird.

Close-up of Bird Teaching Friends to Fly (on page 3) by Laura Balombini. Photo by Robert Diamonte.

Laura Balombini

Over the last few years, Laura Balombini's work has taken a dramatic leap. Something incredibly poetic has occurred. Her work has transformed from clever craft-work to fine art in an incredibly short time. The most obvious change is the addition of wire. Somehow the choice of mediums has refined the expression. "Steel wire and polymer clay are unusual partners, but the soft playfulness of the clay contrasted against the hard, dark lines of the steel work together to form a playful yet serious narrative," Laura explains. This is a delightful surprise and a credit to Laura's vision to explore new expression.

Laura's talent has always been exceptional. In fact, four years ago, I couldn't imagine her art being much better. Laura works in polymer clay and has created some of the most intriguing and clever compositions, drawing on combinations of black and white caned checkers, little people, and "fun things." She fashioned teapots, pins, and pendants. Her art became more conceptually dynamic with the integration of transferred images, butterflies, collaged personalities, and box-framed features. The latest addition of steel wire catapulted Laura's work into a completely new dimension. In my opinion, it is pure, fine art.

Laura also acknowledges that things have definitely changed. Originally, women who appreciate wearable art and the charm of humor in a presentation sought her work. Since her craft became sculpture, it has drawn a more sophisticated audience. The art is now considered an investment as opposed to a "collected item." Sculpture attracts a more serious critic. The materials are not as important as the art. This is a goal artisans

Wire in Design

working in polymer clay have striven for during the last two decades. Wire, which is also non-traditional as an art medium, curiously appeals to a customer who was not anticipated: men. Laura, who travels to art shows throughout New England, discussed how men in particular are drawn to the metal aspect of the sculpture; they are more convinced to invest in sculpture than wearable art or teapots.

Laura hints that her inspiration comes from antique shops and the old wireware from Italy and France. I think the inspiration comes from her sense of humor. Does anyone care to play on the Boing Boing Chess Set?

Circus Pyramid by Laura Balombini. Photo by Jeff Baird.

■ ■ ■ ■ ■ ■

"Steel wire and polymer clay are unusual partners, but the soft playfulness of the clay contrasted against the hard, dark lines of the steel work together to form a playful yet serious narrative."

--Laura Balombini

Storyteller by Laura Balombini. Photo by Bob Barrett.

Sherie Yazman

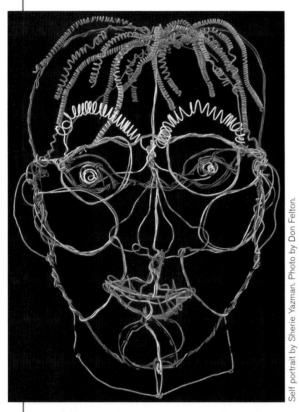

Self portrait by Sherie Yazman. Photo by Don Felton.

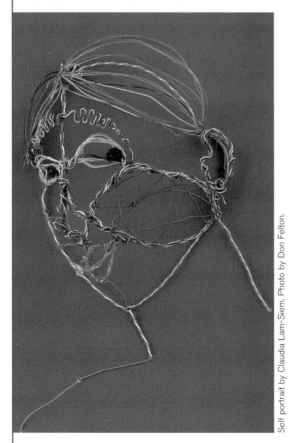

Self portrait by Claudia Lam-Siem. Photo by Don Felton.

The Youth Arts Festival is an annual event held at the DeYoung Museum in Golden Gate Park, San Francisco. While strolling through the museum, I came upon a collection of excellent wire portraits. This was a youth exhibit, but the pieces looked professional. I learned that the portraits were the work of high school students taught by Sherie Yazman, who has been teaching art for nearly twenty years.

The portraits I had seen were made of Internet connection cables; the project came about because Sherie had the foresight to make something wonderful out of material that was designated for the garbage. Her art room was assigned as the Internet hub for the entire school. Sherie was concerned about the traffic and potential damage to the art and equipment in her room and lobbied to have additional storage. Her negotiations helped to make a productive situation of the experience. The installation required 100-foot length cables, and the short pieces were tossed away. Sherie and other teachers immediately claimed the wire. Her entire budget for 300 students during the course of one year is $300; the cable is worth one dollar per foot! This made retrieving the wire a worthwhile endeavor.

Sherie begins by instructing her students to create self portraits in pencil on the backside of a mat board. The students add dimension and form to the two-dimensional portraits with wire. Their individual preference with the tactile medium encourages unique expression in the overall project. Many of the portraits are braided, twisted, and curled, which add movement and texture to the pieces. The colors are also a personal choice, and Sherie encourages realistic proportion in the portraits. My favorite works, however, are the more abstract portraits. The students are from all nationalities, and it is amazing how much each portrait looks like the student. They will undoubtedly learn valuable art concepts from their experience in drawing and sculpture with wire. I am sure Sherie will find additional ways to use wire, as well as other found objects!

Wire in Design

In May 2000, Sherie's students won a Silver Key Award of Scholastic Achievement for the portrait project.

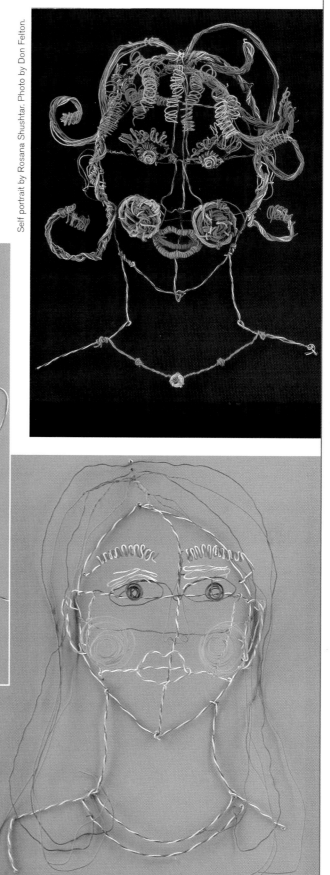

Self portrait by Rosana Shushtar. Photo by Don Felton.

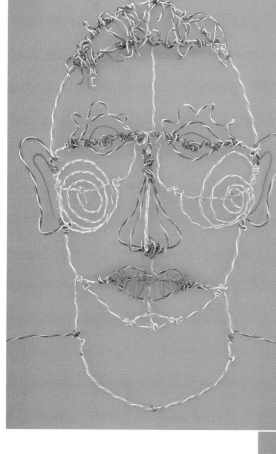

Self portrait by Vlad Gavrilyuk. Photo by Don Felton.

Self portrait by Amy Jin Yu Kuang. Photo by Don Felton.

Wire As an Art Medium

These whimsical wire portraits were inspired by Alexander Calder's wire face mobiles. They are not only wonderful to look at for their sculptural quality, but also for the delightful cast shadows that occur as light shines on them from various angles. The portraits are like contour drawings, only the lines are created with wire instead of a pen or pencil.

■ Materials ■

Colored mat board, approximately 11" x 14"
Scrap telephone or Internet wire (plastic-coated copper wire) in various colors
Flush cutters or old scissors
Pencil
Masking or Scotch tape
Awl or sharp pointed instrument
Optional: bamboo skewers, chopsticks
Colored mat board for framing finished work

1. On the back of the mat board, draw a 1/2" border around the edges. This will give you sufficient space for the final matting when the portrait is completed.

2. Draw a face on the back side of the board, using the correct proportions of the human face as guidelines. It is not necessary to draw in great detail, only the general features, including ears, a small portion of the neck, and some of the shoulder line. These areas will be used to anchor the wire on the front of the board as you begin the project.

3. With an awl or sharp pointed instrument, poke small holes at the top of the head and at the top and bottom of the ears. Poke a hole at the top and bottom on each side of the neck. You will need a few more holes at the ends of the shoulders. Be careful not to push the sharp instrument too far because it will leave large, unattractive holes showing through the face. You may wish to include a few more holes if the face has a hairstyle that sticks out beyond the top of

Self portrait by Claudia Lam-Siem. Photo by Don Felton.

the head (many hairstyles can be created by adding wire to the basic structure and do not require the extra holes). **Note:** Try to keep the number of holes to a minimum so that most of the work is done by manipulating the wire on the front of the board.

4. Prepare the wire by stripping away the outer plastic coating that covers the bundles of copper wire inside. Use lengths of wire no more than 3 feet long at a time to avoid tangling. Cut the thin colored wire with flush cutters or an old scissors to desired lengths.

5. For a strong face foundation, begin by twisting two 3-foot lengths of wire together. Put this wire into the hole on the top of the head and pull through to the front of the board. Tie a knot at the end of the wire on the back of the board and secure it with a piece of tape. The face is made on the front of the board by creating a large loop of wire, inserting it back into the top hole, and securing it to the back. The loop should be a little larger than the size of the face drawing. The extra length will shrink as you begin to connect the wire at the anchor points.

6. At the top of the ear holes, loop a shorter length of wire from the back of the board to the front. Catch the face wire in the loop before pulling the wire to the back. Knot and tape the end of the wire to the board. With the same wire, repeat the looping process at the bottom ear hole, again catching the face wire in the loop before pulling it back down to the back. Now the face wire should be held down in place at the ear anchor points.

7. Bring the wire back up to the top ear hole and create a loop on the front to make the shape of the ear lobe. Poke the wire back into the bottom of the ear hole, knot, and tie the wire to the back side. Repeat this process for the other ear.

8. Continue to secure the face wire at the neck anchor holes with a new length of twisted wire. Finish drawing the neck and shoulder lines with the wire until you get the desired image. Knot and cut the wire when you are finished, putting tape over the knot to prevent unraveling.

9. Begin to add colored wires to the front of the face to fill in the "drawing." Like a contour drawing, you want to connect all of the wire parts together like one continuous line. Start by wrapping single or twisted wires to the side of the temple area of the head and bring the wire across the face and begin to form an eye. Continue with the same length of wire and make the other eye. Wrap the wire to the other side of the head to secure this building structure to the face. Wrap wire back to the center between the eyes and build the nose structure. You may wish to create the lips from a separate wire and connect them to the nose, so you form one unit with the eyes, nose, and lips. The face becomes more whimsical as you add details like eyelids, brows, eyeballs, and maybe even glasses. Try to make the face three-dimensional as you work on the front of the board. If you turn the board sideways, you can also see the face's profile. Build out the forehead, nose, cheeks, lip, and chin areas.

10. Complete the portrait by adding wire hair. Hair can be made by wrapping wire tightly around chopsticks or bamboo skewers, giving it a curly texture. Try making zigzags or pinching the wire for interesting effects. Make sure you weave or wrap added wires to the face structure securely so they won't come loose.

11. Use the remaining piece of colored mat board to frame the piece.

■ ■ ■ ■ ■ ■ ■

Creating a portrait of wire is an intriguing work. One line or profile can capture the personality of the subject. The structure can be flat or incorporate any amount of dimension. Space is an integral element of the design.

Mask by Tina DeWeese. Photo by Tina DeWeese.

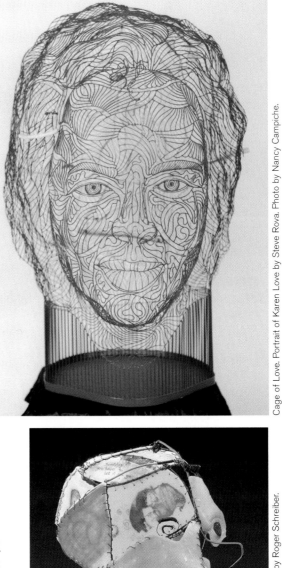

Cage of Love. Portrait of Karen Love by Steve Rova. Photo by Nancy Campiche.

Wire Bird Cage. Self portrait by Steve Rova. Photo by Mary Campiche.

Clay and wire portrait sculpture by Meredeth Arnold. Photo by Roger Schreiber.

WIRE AS ADORNMENT

*M*any years ago, people began to embrace jewelry as the venue for wearing art. This freedom brought about the ability for collectors to enjoy and accessorize their wardrobes by abandoning traditional precious metals and gems. Today, a piece of polymer clay connected by telephone wire can be as valuable as a sapphire, a pearl, or—dare I compare—a diamond. The adornment is valuable because of the art. Wire sculpture is sculpture. The fact that it is functional as a wearable piece is irrelevant to its value, but it is a delightful bonus. Ancient adornment is now treasured as the artifacts of the nations. The true value comes in the creativ-

Gold ensemble with purple seed beads by Cynthia Darling.

ity, craftsmanship, and composition of the piece, something that can be enjoyed both on and off the wearer. It is also something that is attained in any medium, including wire.

Many of the artists profiled in this chapter could be painters or sculptors. They are no less artists because they are creating wearable art. Each uses the elements and principles of design to strengthen their work. Perhaps because of the visibility of their work, they enjoy an audience greater than that of traditional artists. And because of their talent, we can use that creativity to enhance our own persona.

Sterling bracelets and enamel piece by Cynthia Darling.

Wire as Adornment

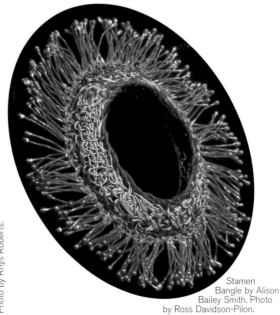

lison Bailey Smith may not have intended to make hats when she enrolled in the Edinburgh College of Art, but she definitely intended to flourish as an innovative artist. Her schooling encompassed artistic and technical aspects of jewelry production, which later enabled her to conceive and construct jewelry. Since 1988, her jewelry and other wearable art have successfully incorporated recycled materials. Her techniques are reminiscent of brocade and filigree work, although it is not immediately obvious that the material is wire. Her works with recycled materials, primarily wire, become a subtle statement of modern times. "By emphasizing the value of design, my hope has been to offer an alternative to the conservative convention of only viewing precious jewelry as an investment commodity," Smith states of her work.

The titles of exhibitions, publications, and collections that Smith has participated in reflect the innovative nature of her audience: FIRE, Jewellery Moves, Techno Cannibal, Wired for Wear, Metal Urges, Metal Millinery, Mad About Hats, and Twisted—the list goes on and on, and

Spire Hat and Bolero by Alison Bailey Smith.
Photo by Rhys Roberts.

Stamen Bangle by Alison Bailey Smith. Photo by Ross Davidson-Pilon.

also includes more traditional credits such as the Platinum Award Touring Exhibition. Alison has displayed her work in exhibitions throughout the British Isles, Canada, and Australia. In 1991, she was named the Scottish Fashion Designer of the Year, followed by Recycling Designer of the Year (UK) in 1992.

What are Alison's innovative fashions made of? TV wire. I was shocked to learn Alison had such a "hands on" approach. She states, "All of the wire used in the pieces has been recycled by me. It takes an hour to gut a television and a week to make a hat. Each piece is lined for comfort and designed to be worn. Each creation is unique and can never be repeated exactly the same."

■　　■　　■　　■　　■　　■

Alison's techniques are reminiscent of brocade and filigree work, although it is not immediately obvious that the material is wire.

Embossed Pill Box Hat by Alison Bailey Smith. Photo by Ross Davidson-Pilon.

Flame Collar by Alison Bailey Smith. Photo by Ross Davidson-Pilon.

■ ■ ■ ■ ■

Woven wire is a phenomenon that carries a unique intrigue. The skills of the weaver combined with the character of the wire create stunning works. The applied techniques develop pattern and rhythm throughout the piece. Skills such as knitting, crochet, weaving, and basketry can be expressed with the delicate wire being manufactured today. The availability of specific metals, colors, and finishes gives artists a wondrous palette.

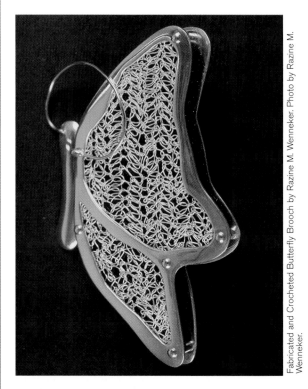

Fabricated and Crocheted Butterfly Brooch by Razine M. Wenneker. Photo by Razine M. Wenneker.

Crocheted wire bags with blown glass and ceramic adornment by Pat Moses-Caudel. Photo by Almac Camera.

Crocheted wire bags by fashion designer Lisa Toland. Photo by Almac Camera.

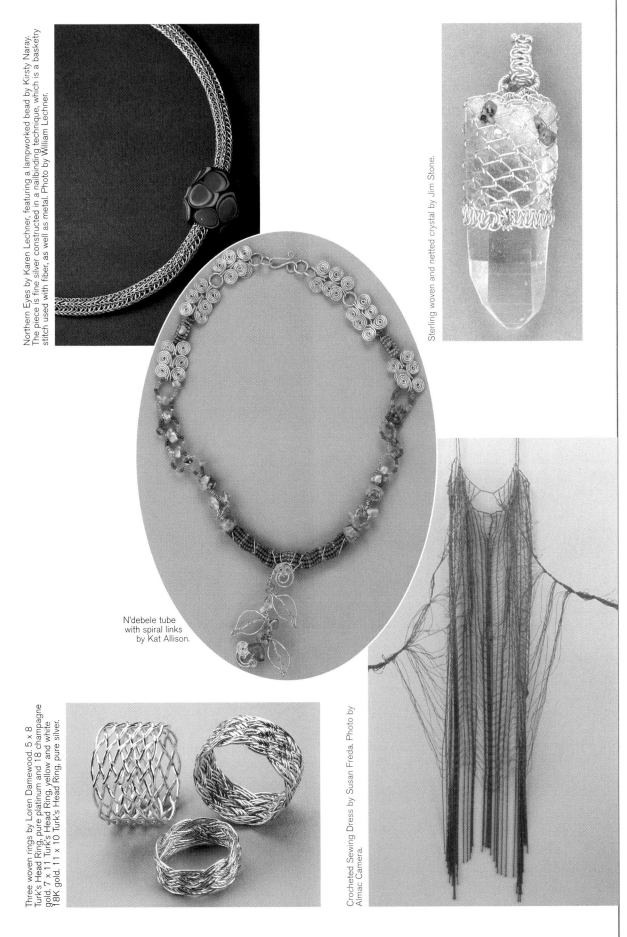

Northern Eyes by Karen Lechner, featuring a lampworked bead by Kirsty Naray. The piece is fine silver constructed in a nailbinding technique, which is a basketry stitch used with fiber, as well as metal. Photo by William Lechner.

Sterling woven and netted crystal by Jim Stone.

N'debele tube with spiral links by Kat Allison.

Three woven rings by Loren Damewood. 5 x 8 Turk's Head Ring, pure platinum and 18 champagne gold. 7 x 11 Turk's Head Ring, yellow and white 18K gold. 11 x 10 Turk's Head Ring, pure silver.

Crocheted Sewing Dress by Susan Freda. Photo by Almac Camera.

Wire as Adornment

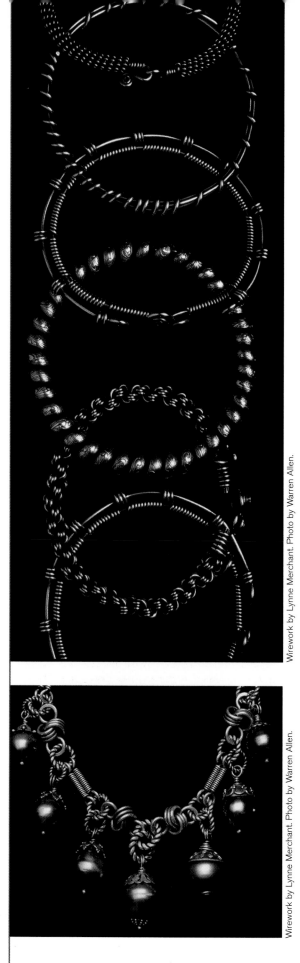

Wirework by Lynne Merchant. Photo by Warren Allen.

Wirework by Lynne Merchant. Photo by Warren Allen.

Lynne Merchant

$\mathcal{L}$ynne Merchant's artistry in wire speaks for itself. She has worked with wire for thirty years, and the admirer easily recognizes that she has complete mastery of her craft and is free to design what her mind sees.

Her imagination was shaped as a young girl, when she coiled her father's pipe cleaners, and has blossomed into a style that is immediately recognized and held in awe. Lynne's sense of design reflects her worldly travels and the rhythm of age-old traditions learned at the foot of master artisans. She adds to that technical knowledge her incredible patience and perseverance—and her desire to keep evolving in her craft.

In discovering Lynne's art, I was fascinated by the essence of a rare beauty: the soul in hand-work. Lynne considers herself a purist, and she works with a simple set of tools. Her most important tool by far is her own body, and the closer you look at her personal tools, the more you realize that they are made to perform as an extension of her body.

When you look closely at her art, you see the elegance and refinement she brings to the process. I found that while attending Lynne's classes, the closer one pays attention, the more one is empowered. For me, there will always be a clear delineation between my art before I met Lynne Merchant and my art after meeting her. It is amazing that one person can influence so profoundly. Lynne gives her students much more than just a class about making wire beads, or baskets, or bracelets. She gives insights that she has gleaned from her experience and her mistakes. If you allow that kind of sharing to sink in, it changes you.

I sought to speak to Lynne because she has influenced so many artists, and her work is reflected in many pieces of wire art I have seen. I wondered what Lynne would think about seeing her work duplicated by people she had never met. With this in mind, I contacted her to ask

Wirework by Lynne Merchant. Photo by Warren Allen.

for an interview. Lynne, wisely, suggested that I take one of her classes in order to understand who she is and what she is about. In addition to the incredible instruction—much of which is included in this book—we had conversations about creativity, intention, and passion. I went away with a deepened understanding of what motivates a person to produce art, and about the essence of a fine piece of handwork.

Lynne works in silver. All of her work is done by hand. All of it. Yes, she uses small manual tools, but her hands have also touched every centimeter of metal. She has worked the silver wire into a strength that is right for the object she is creating. This thoroughness reflects the blending of her education at the California College of Arts and Crafts and her life experiences. Lynne insists that a piece of wirework be structurally sound as well as interesting. It must rely on engineering to make it strong. The strength of the work is seen in an instant. Many of Lynne's pieces are significant in size. I realized how small I had been working. I realized how small I had been thinking.

Each bead Lynne makes is a new creation. There is a spark of something she has absorbed; an idea, a discovery, or a memory in each one. All of her beads are named to acknowledge the inspiration or to commemorate the occasion. Alexander Calder has had a profound influence

on her work, and the basic spiral bead Lynne begins her lessons with is entitled the Calder Coil. The Kuchi bead was inspired by her many trips to Afghanistan in the '70s, where she collected ethnic jewelry and absorbed many ancient techniques from master artisans. Other beads are humorously named, such as the Croissant bead and the Saturn bead. Naming the beads gives them an identity; they are no longer just a project—each one has a birth and a personality.

Lynne stresses to her students that they should take the techniques she teaches and reach deep inside themselves to add their own creative design. She hopes they will nourish the activity of their own imagination. She encourages them to process the class and learn the techniques, not just to attempt to turn out a copied product. She often quotes Eleanor Roosevelt, who said, "No one was ever great by imitation." Lynne stresses that we, the students, should keep our early student creations as our personal treasures, as symbols of our own personal creative journey.

The first class Lynne recommends for a new student is called Findings, which she describes as "the bare bones of wire bending." Lynne believes that the techniques she teaches are like the letters of an alphabet, which can make up words, sentences, and whole stories. "Findings are like prepositions," she says, "they hold the sentence together."

Wirework by Lynne Merchant. Photo by Warren Allen.

Many students, after taking a few classes, are so stimulated by what they've learned that they are tempted to reproduce and sell their student work. Some even attempt to reproduce her classes. This brings us back to the original question of what Lynne thinks about seeing her work duplicated. How do you learn something and resist the temptation to copy? That's pretty hard to resist. It's even harder to get the image out of your head after you have been influenced by it—it can even crop up years later as your own original design. "In the beginning, my students learn skills by imitation," Lynne says, "but the ones who go on to become wire artists add their own creative muscle to their skill."

How does Lynne feel about sharing her knowledge? Giving up her hard-learned techniques was a diffi-cult decision for her to make. She had care-fully guarded the knowledge she had acquired over many years. But in 1987, she made a con-scious decision to be a teacher, something that she takes quite seriously. Lynne believes that "Knowledge comes from books, but understanding comes from experience." She tries to

give her students an experience from which they can gain understanding, rather than a recipe for a project.

Once Lynne has designed and created a piece of jewelry, she is often reluctant to sell it, because she has put so much of her soul into it, and, as she says, "How much is your soul worth?" So Lynne teaches. Her classes are in demand and are always full. Most of her work-shops are held at The Shepherdess in San Diego, CA, and at Beads and Beyond in Bellevue, WA. Students travel from all over the country to attend her classes because teachers like Lynne tailor instruction to the individual student.

In recent years, Lynne has become fascinated with Tahitian black pearls. It is not surprising, because their odd shapes and myriad of colors lend themselves to a curious blending with sil-ver wire. She likes to see what she can do with the odd, maverick pearl, the one that seems to have a story all its own. The challenge is to secure them with silver while preserving their individual character. Learning about pearls, like learning about wire, has required travel. Lynne travels to the atolls of Tahiti to experience the pearl harvests and to better understand the properties of the pearls with which she works.

I learned from Lynne that good art, like good advice, is hard earned. You have to make all the mistakes to get it right. It takes time, concen-tration, and invest-ment. But more than that it takes the confidence to know that you can do it on your own, that you don't need to be someone else… or his or her art. The essence of the person unfolds in his or her handwork. The more I understand this, the more I treasure the things I possess

Wirework by Lynne Merchant. Photo by Warren Allen.

Wire in Design

that people have made by hand. I treasure my newfound friend, who has taught me many things. I also understand that I had been so busy trying to *use* my talent that I had neglected to *be* my talent. Indeed, I came back to San Francisco not only with Lynne's wire as I had expected, but with a foundation on which to build my own future in wire. I came back with a pearl; not only a black pearl, but also a pearl of revelation that can change my world and my art. I can only say thank you to Lynne for giving so freely of her rare and exceptional gifts.

■   ■   ■   ■   ■   ■

I learned from Lynne that good art, like good advice, is hard earned. You have to make all the mistakes to get it right. It takes time, concentration, and investment. But more than that it takes the confidence to know that you can do it on your own, that you don't need to be someone else… or his or her art.

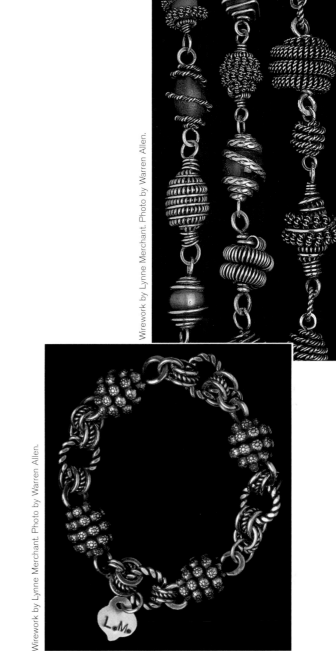

Wirework by Lynne Merchant. Photo by Warren Allen.

Wirework by Lynne Merchant. Photo by Warren Allen.

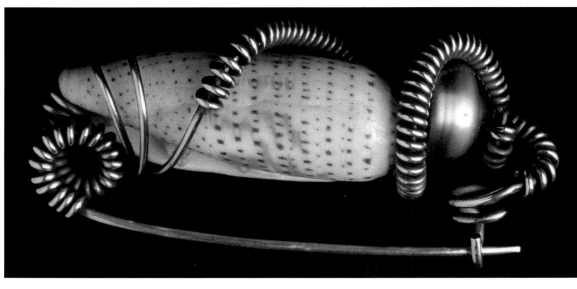

Wirework by Lynne Merchant. Photo by Warren Allen.

Copper Necklace 1 with lampworked glass beads by Barbara Becker Simon. Photo by Rob Stegman.

Barbara Becker Simon

Barbara Becker Simon is incredibly motivated and diversely talented. She began her career with professional schooling in art education and found her devotion gravitating toward jewelry making. That interest encouraged Barbara to keep pursuing her talents, and she received an MFA from the distinguished metalsmithing program at the University of Wisconsin. After graduating, she taught at universities for seven years and then retired in 1978 to a small Wisconsin town to raise her daughter; however, she continued to do commissioned work.

After making jewelry for thirty years, Barbara jumped at the chance to take a class with Lynne Merchant (see page 58), whose methods for wirework are straightforward,

■ ■ ■ ■ ■

Barbara's work is extremely elegant but at the same time she can create pieces with common appeal; she describes her work as sophisticated and technically complicated.

Bubble Bead Necklace, wire and glass beads by Barbara Becker Simon. Photo by Rob Stegman.

simple, and allow the artist a technical liberation. After years of complicated steps involved to get a piece of jewelry, Lynne's "no soldering, no buffing, no filing" handwork opened the doors of freedom. The results are immediate, incredibly fun, and rewarding. Barbara adds the distinction of her own glass lampworked beads to Lynne's basic approach to create her own style and techniques. Barbara's work is extremely elegant but at the same time she can create pieces with common appeal; she describes her work as sophisticated and technically complicated.

Her marching ant glass beads won a first place award at Embellishment, the Bead & Button Show, in 1999. "A lot of the pieces in a high-end range are too esoteric, and a broader audience is served by something more relatable," Barbara says in discussion of her "ants." With wire, she can expand her theme to embrace the limitless variety of her personal creations, lampworked glass, and, most recently, Precious Metal Clay beads and components. The wire helps to create a rhythm and unity throughout the work.

"I am able to dream up some wire elements that are just right for certain problem areas in the jewelry." Barbara explains. "I like the immediacy and the freedom. I also like the linear quality that is inherent in the form of wire and the fact that these 'lines' can be formed into 'solid' objects. To some pieces it gives an airy quality, to others, a more solid look. Lots of variation in wire usage is an advantage. It is like a puzzle to work out some of the design, which is a fun way to approach making jewelry."

Wirework sampler with lampworked glass beads by Barbara Becker Simon. Photo by Rob Stegman.

Lavender Bubble Bead Necklace, sterling, glass, pearls, and amethyst by Barbara Becker Simon. Photo by Rob Stegman.

Wire as Adornment

Freeform design with wire allows the character of wire to have an impact on the design. Many artists prefer to respond to the flow of the wire rather than dictate it. Bends, loops, and twists give the line element movement and rhythm.

Macramé knotted necklace with wrapped wire headpiece by Diane Hyde. Photo by Jay Jones.

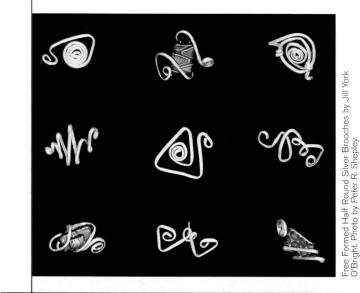

Free Formed Half Round Silver Brooches by Jill York O'Bright. Photo by Peter R. Shepley.

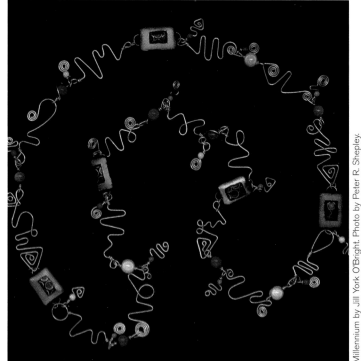

Millennium by Jill York O'Bright. Photo by Peter R. Shepley.

Freeform necklace by Linda Muscante, with Glass Headbead by Karen Ovington.

Pier Voulkos

Looking at the work of Pier Voulkos makes you feel like a kid in a candy store. It evokes delightful and enchanting memories from a playful place or time. But make no mistake; this is no toy—this is serious art. Pier is a genius in control of form, shape, and color, not to mention rhythm and unity. Viewing her work is one big art lesson rolled into one. Every time I leave her company, I want to immediately disregard my personal schedule and make something colorful.

The presence of wire in her work began in the late 1980s. She first used telephone wire to wire patterned shrink art charms and polymer clay slices for her neckpieces between 1985 and 1986. A couple of years later, when trying to make earrings, she discovered that telephone wire could be securely baked into polymer clay.

Pier perfects a particular style over a period of months, even years, so you can be assured that the technical execution of the art is sound. She creates themes in series that often integrate and evolve into the next season or subsequent years. The progression of her work is fascinating and amazing. In any particular focus, she will repeat the same form or shape but will apply it with a different style. In doing so, she creates unique pieces that are similar and related but always have a fresh energy. The essence that remains intact throughout the evolution in the art is the identifying character of the artist. Many artists strive for a "trademark" style. Pier has been successful in creating a trademark of colorful innovation, passing on the technique of her work and encouraging countless students to seek their own expression, combining polymer clay with wire.

Wire and clay caned necklace by Pier Volkous. Photo by George Post.

Wire and shrink art necklace by Pier Volkous. Photo by George Post.

Similar to many of the artists currently attracted to wire, Pier made wire jewelry as a kid. Telephone wire used to be a common recyclable material, an inexpensive material for children's use. During her teen years, as a children's art and craft teacher, she used it for many children's projects.

Pier began wiring baked polymer clay slices for earrings, looking to add movement and interest. She wanted dangling parts to wiggle; to do that she needed them to hang off of some sort of hook or staple. With metal wire she would have to glue the hooks individually into the baked clay. When she found she could bake the PVC wire hooks into the clay, that was the perfect solution: it allowed for quick, effective production by hooking and baking pre-baked and wired cane slices onto a raw slice of clay for the earring base. This opened up the world to all sorts of earring designs. She developed an eye screw system for beads, adding extra clay folded over the hole to lock the screw in, which gives added security and strength over a staple system.

I asked her about the multitudes of tiny pieces. How did she remain sane in the cascade of color? How could she do all of the details at once? As production work, she could farm this work out, but not far. Her husband, Dan Peters, an exceptional wood design artist, does the production wiring. Today, Pier and Dan often collaborate in their work, as well as teach their innovative techniques.

Clay and wire earrings with stand by Pier Volkous. Photo by George Post.

Bracelet by Pier Volkous; the beads are attached with wire. Photo by George Post.

Most telephone wire is copper wire with a colorful, striped PVC coating, a perfect complement to colorful polymer clay. You must be cautious because not all colorful plastic-looking wire is PVC-coated; some may have a nylon coating. Polymer clay is primarily PVC with a plasticizer that keeps it malleable until heated. Popularly known by brand names—FIMO, Sculpey, and Premo—polymer clay permanently hardens at temperatures of 265° (brands may vary in manufacturers' suggested baking requirements). For extra strength, the clay must be well cured. Pier uses a convection oven to bump up the temperature to 300° for just a moment and then lets pieces cool before handling. This is something you cannot do in a toaster oven, because the direct heat will toast the clay, and additional venting of fumes should be considered. Monitoring internal oven temperatures is a must and can be done with basic oven thermometers. Before you begin your project, test the wire to assure it can withstand baking temperatures.

■ ■ ■ ■ ■ ■

Cascades of polymer clay beads are well served by using poly-coated wire as a connecting design element. The wire is embedded or woven into the beads and keep continuity in the materials used. The PVC coating on the wire adheres to the clay, enforcing the structural strength of the piece.

Leaves by Nancy Banks, created with polymer clay, transfer foils, and wire.

Purses and Shoes by Deborah Anderson. Photo by Liv Ames.

Oceania by Ann Mitchell of AnKara Designs. Photo by Ai Buangsuwon.

Collar of Faunas necklace by Karen Mitchell of AnKara Designs, created with wire, beads, fabric, and liquid clay transfer techniques. Photo by Ai Buangsuwon.

Wire as Adornment

Linda Goff

I asked Linda Goff, "What came first? The clay or the wire?" She explained, "Well, I used to work in metal and enamel." Lucky for us, Linda fell in love with polymer clay; she is known for her delightful animals, fish, and birds, reflecting an influence of the Pacific Northwest. She finds animals and nature more interesting than abstract design. Her pieces usually end in a spiral or zigzag as part of the animal body. Linda also adds textured shapes of clay to define the character's form.

But the clay presented a problem that she needed to solve. Linda wanted to get a nice edge on the pieces. "Nice" is an understatement; she means beautiful, striking, and complementary to the whole. At first, Linda considered smooth wire, but that wouldn't work because it wouldn't stick to the clay. Linda solved her obstacle by wrapping the smooth wire with an extremely fine colored wire and embellishing it with beads. There is a beautiful rhythm in the borders of her handwork. It takes nearly a half an hour to complete an outline of a small piece. Linda said wrapping is a spontaneous part of the creation, and she anticipates the design elements as she

wraps. Indeed, the tiny beads add enough contrast to bring attention to the border, and the variation in the wrap moves the eye through the piece. "I chose wire because I love the contrast of the cold wire with the warm clay," Linda declares. She enjoys the fairly realistic colors of wire available on the market, and she is able to mix her own clay color palette.

Linda never took a wire class and just started experimenting on her own. Initially, she sold pieces at art shows and waited about nine years before she taught her technique. As soon as she was ready to move on in her work, she was prompted to share her technique. Linda began teaching at conferences and guilds, at which she still encourages others to "run with it." Linda says she learns from her students and wants to start a collection of their work. "I think kids would also like to try this," Linda encourages. "I had a child in a class once and it went really well."

Although she is recognized for her wire animal characters, Linda doesn't feel pigeon-holed. Her interest in new techniques has recently prompted exploration in metals and foils, but she always comes back to using wire in her work.

Brooches by Linda Goff. These examples reflect her signature style and themes.

"I chose wire because I love the contrast of the cold wire with the warm clay"   --Linda Goff

Even though artists learn from each other, if you allow yourself enough freedom, an individual style will emerge. Often, we are afraid to allow our creativity to develop because we do not wish to copy our teacher. I believe Nan Roche, author of *The New Clay*, elegantly and accurately defined a copy as "art using the same techniques, same themes or images, same shapes and colors." The artists presented have taken a basic wrapped edge technique and developed their own personal expression. The work reflects the technique but clearly has the mark of the individual artists.

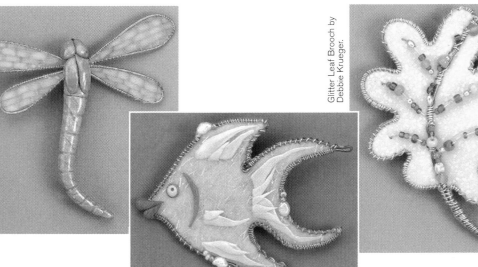

Caned Heart Brooch by Kim Korringa.

Wild Spirit by Jean Comport.

Impressed Leaf Brooch by Kim Korringa.

Gold Leaf Inclusion Dragonfly Brooch by Debbie Krueger.

Glitter Leaf Brooch by Debbie Krueger.

Glitter Confetti Fish Brooch by Debbie Krueger.

Wire as Adornment

■ ■ ■ ■ ■ ■ ■

Wire as a single line element can have incredible impact. Whether it is drawn or contained within a work or used as a component in a complete composition, it is still a line. It has the ability to lead the eye through the work or around the neck, as a singular line element in a piece of jewelry. When you are writing with wire, the line becomes the image of a word and transforms into direct communication.

Wire-wrapped steel strand with pendant by M.J. Bennett. Photo by Almac Camera.

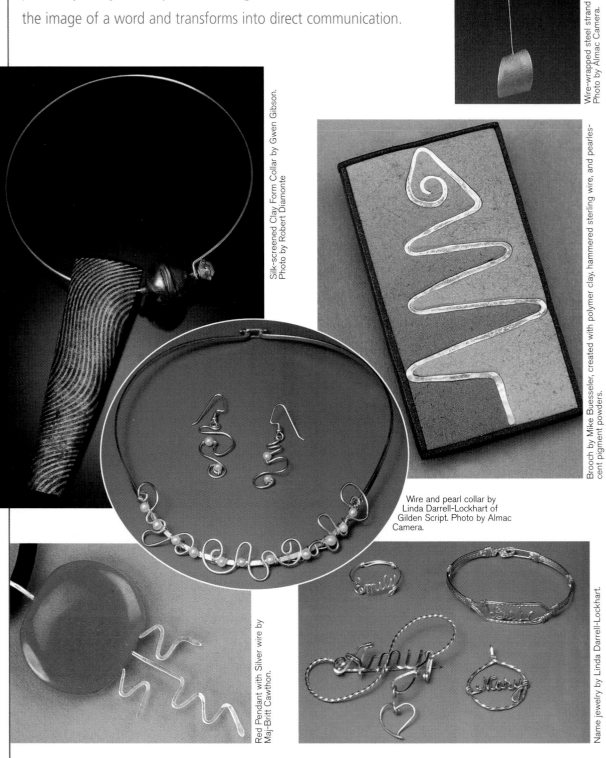

Silk-screened Clay Form Collar by Gwen Gibson. Photo by Robert Diamonte

Brooch by Mike Buesseler, created with polymer clay, hammered sterling wire, and pearlescent pigment powders.

Wire and pearl collar by Linda Darrell-Lockhart of Gilden Script. Photo by Almac Camera.

Red Pendant with Silver wire by Maj-Britt Cawthon.

Name jewelry by Linda Darrell-Lockhart.

Preston Reuther

Preston Reuther is a master wire sculptor. His title reflects his engagement with wire sculpture, the art of setting stones in swirls, loops, and wraps of square wire, usually gold. It is a popular alternative to traditional gem settings and incorporates the artistry of the jeweler.

Preston hasn't kept this art to himself; instead, it is his vision to empower anyone to discover his or her own creativity in this medium. He had not considered himself an artist and was astounded when he discovered he could create beautiful jewelry. The stones are a personal choice, and the style is individual. I sent Preston a picture of the square wire project I had made (see Project 8, page 122). He responded, "I never saw anything like that." That's just an indication of what I mean by personal "style."

Preston has a large Internet audience that seeks advice and posts pictures of art (www.wire-sculpture.com). The group shares, and discussions include the mistakes and troubles the artists are having getting wire to perform, as well as how to market work and please customers. Making jewelry for oneself is one thing, but making it for the public assumes some responsibility. You learn when people bring things back that have fallen apart or have snagged clothes that your workmanship and awareness need to improve!

One of my favorite discussions was about an ugly piece of jewelry (to this I could totally relate). The following story is a sample of Preston's honest advice:

"Everyone makes ugly jewelry from time to time, even if you're a seasoned professional. The important thing is how do we deal with it and what do we do with that ugly piece of jewelry. Lots of artists that I know of will destroy all of their ugly pieces because they want nothing to do with them. But I rarely do that anymore because several years ago something very interesting happened to me. I was working in my studio at a furious pace so an important order for a sales rep would be ready the following morning. About midnight I was just about finished making some sculpted pieces in silver when I broke one of the settings. I got so frustrated I

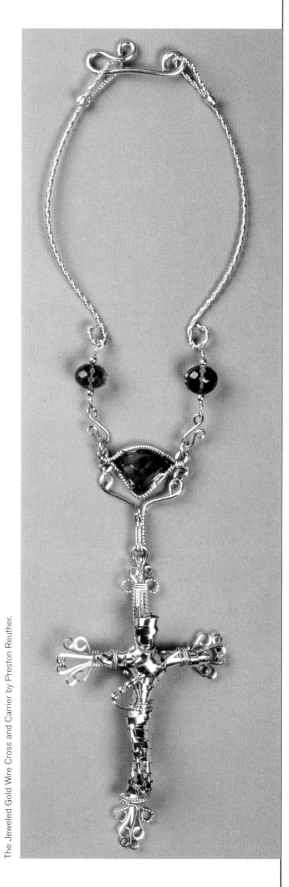

The Jeweled Gold Wire Cross and Carrier by Preston Reuther.

smashed it with my rawhide hammer! To make a long story short, the next morning the customer came over to pick up his order. His eye caught the flattened sterling silver setting. He looked at it, picked it up, and asked how much? It took everything I had to keep a straight face as I said '$20.' He agreed to buy it and left with his order. The next day, he stopped by and wanted to place another order. I took out my receipt book and he said, 'Boy, the shops really like that new **flat design**. Can you give me ten more of those?' The moral of the story? Just be patient, take your time, and soon enough those ugly ducklings will turn into beautiful swans! Where else can you get paid for making mistakes while learning your skill? And there is always the chance that some-one may just fall in love with that ugly duckling, and, who knows, it just might be the beginning of a new design for you."

Preston, I've put your website in my "favorite" places.

Bracelet Watch by Ann Turpin Thayer. Photo by Raymond M. Thayer.

■ ■ ■ ■ ■ ■

Tip from Preston

It's hard to measure wire after you've made a piece, so if you start with a certain length and subtract what's left over, you'll get an idea of how much wire you've used. As well as measuring, you can weigh the finished piece (subtract the weight of any stones) and figure the cost per gram.

■ ■ ■ ■ ■ ■

Another Tip from Preston

Preston says the secret is to work with dead soft wire. Hardness is measured by what is known as the B and S rate: half-hard wire equals a #2 hardness, where #2 means that the wire has been pulled or drawn two times through the draw plate. Hardness extends to #8, which produces spring-hard or pin-hard wire. Each application dictates the required temper or hardness of the wire. Ninety percent of Preston's wire sculpture is done with 14/20K, 21 gauge dead soft wire, which is recommended for creating cascading swirls.

Each project may necessitate more than one gauge and temper. Wire wrapping to hold the stones in place requires a hard or half-hard wire, and sculpting the swirls requires dead soft wire. Solid gold wire is innately hard, gold-filled wire is a base metal (such as sterling silver) rolled in thin sheets of gold, and the temper will be relevant to the hardness of the base metal. Confused? That's why it's best left up to the voice of experi-ence. Preston has produced videos so you can see and learn at the same time. Once you've learned basic skills, you can make pendants, rings, earrings, bracelets, collars, and even Christmas ornaments.

■　■　■　■　■　■

With the communication made available through the Internet, artists are able to meet with each other and post pictures of their work. This presents more ideas, techniques, and inspiration to beginners and professionals alike. The wonderful ornaments are winning entries from a contest sponsored by Preston Reuther.

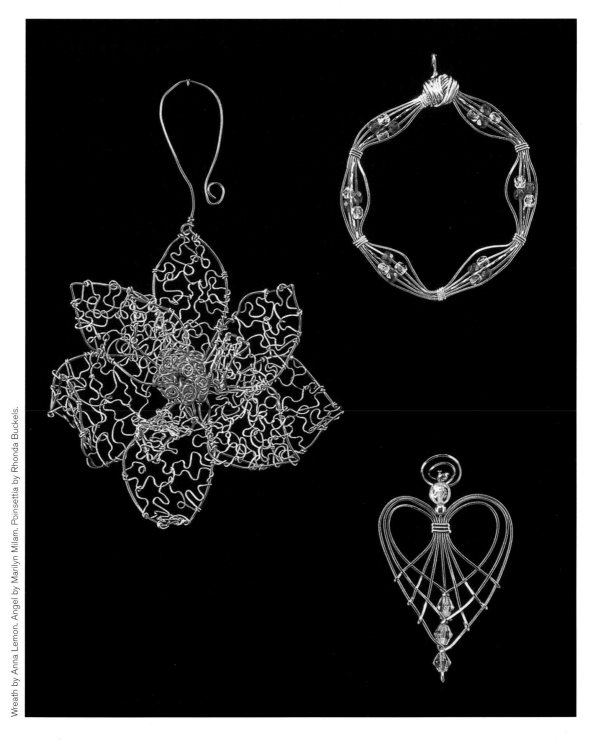

Wreath by Anna Lemon. Angel by Marilyn Milam. Poinsettia by Rhonda Buckels.

Wire as Adornment

The emerging art of wire sculpture promises to expose the talents of many artists, even those not yet discovered. The range in styles and preferences will be as individual as the artists themselves. Wire sculpture gives an artist the ability to set a stone, charm, pearl, or gem as simply or as complex as he or she envisions. Many times, the experimentation is reflected in the piece. The work evolves as it is created. A nontraditional variety of metals and materials are combined to create a dynamic, new look.

Scarf holder of wire and pearls by Barbara A. McGuire. Photo by Jay Jones.

Gold Sculpted Polymer Clay Mokume Gane Bracelet by Dorothy McMillian.

Sculpted wire ring by Mark H. Case, Sr.

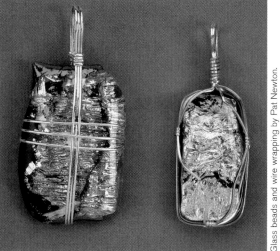

Glass beads and wire wrapping by Pat Newton.

Pendant, wire sculpted by Jerome Bourcy of B.J.'s Creative Wireworks. Photo by Frank Mulligan.

Wire *in* Design

Dianne Karg

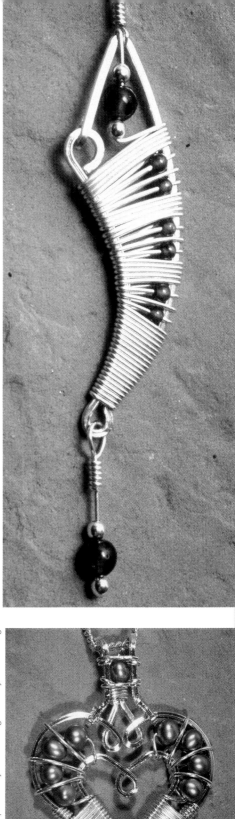

𝓜any times, an artist's statement flies right over me, because I get lost in too many abstract terms and art concepts—an imaginary plane I can't always reach; however, I was struck by Dianne's statement because it expresses something I think many artists are saying: wire art is alive and spontaneous, and it is also a personal, invigorating experience. I gather inspiration from Dianne's unique work and her statement as well:

"For me, making jewelry is an active meditation. I visualize the wire as a sort of three-dimensional line. My inspiration comes from nature, from architecture, from calligraphy, from abstract art—anything that sparks my curiosity. It feels like an exclamation point suddenly igniting in my head. The energy, the rapture, of the inspiration gets channeled from my head, through my spine, through my hands, into the wire in a patient contemplation as I construct the piece. I allow my intuition to develop the form, letting it grow and change without necessarily imposing a predetermined outcome. Sometimes what comes together in the end is completely different from what inspired the journey, but the passion of the initial vision is still encapsulated and expressed in a refined, clear form."

■ ■ ■ ■ ■

"My inspiration comes from nature, from architecture, from calligraphy, from abstract art—anything that sparks my curiosity."
                                                    --Dianne Karg

Allure Pendant by Dianne Karg. Photo by Dianne Karg.

Smooth Wrapped Series: heart pendant by Dianne Karg. Photo by Dianne Karg.

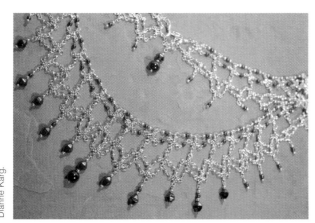

Ode to Canadian Winter by Dianne Karg. Photo by Dianne Karg.

Wendy Witchner

"There's definitely a right and a left," Wendy Witchner states numerous times during our conversation. "The earrings just look better when they are worn a certain way. They look better pointing outward. The little gold wire pieces fall into the pockets between the beads in the necklace, and the pieces look better on than in the box." Wendy is an artist who understands balance in its intended environment. She likes space and asymmetry, exemplifying that less is more. Most of the time, she discussed how the wire looked when it was being *worn*. Indeed, her work resembles a complete wardrobe; there is a piece for every mood and a piece for every taste. Wendy's ability to focus on a theme is revealed in the way she limits the components to emphasize the statement. Her work is very straightforward and elegantly clean.

Wendy travels in a motor home, selling her art across the country at a series of chosen shows. Because of her limited facilities, she invented ways to connect pieces and attach beads without soldering. As a result, the relationship between the wire as a design element and its functional purpose is very striking.

Wendy picked up wire in her early teens, when she had an innate ability to make two pieces the same. Wendy abandoned wire for twenty years and later picked it up again as therapy. She always wanted to take jewelry classes and once was a student of Lynne Merchant (see page 58). She also got a lesson just admiring the work of street artists and started buying pieces of pounded wire

Wire collar and bracelet with vintage glass carved buttons by Wendy Witchner.

Wire in Design

jewelry. Influenced by a street artist in Berkeley, CA, Wendy got her old tools out and created wire chair earrings. She also designed fish earrings by creating an outline of thicker wire and filling in the body with silver wire. Eventually, wire evolved into her chosen medium.

In a former life, Wendy was an airline pilot; she used to fly twin-engine planes. Now she is a road pilot, traveling and working on the road for an entire year at a time. She works for very long stretches of time, usually in groupings. She can do coiled pieces quickly, while bracelets take longer. Wendy incorporates a variety of metals as well as texture. She likes the reflection of texture in a hammered piece. The secret of achieving texture, Wendy informs, is not to pound flat on flat; you need a balteen head that hammers flat. A steel block or anvil does the forming and shaping. To create texture, you must move around the surface of the wire. A heavier hammer is more effective in attaining desired results.

I asked Wendy if she wanted to marry a wire artist. She said she always wanted to marry Mr. Adventure, a risk-taker. She used to be a surfer. Each wave is a new thrill. How does this personality relate to wire? "Wire is under-appreciated; there is always something new you can do with it. How many different ways can you bend a coil? As many ways as you can ride a wave."

■ ■ ■ ■ ■ ■

Wendy's ability to focus on a theme is revealed in the way she limits the components to emphasize the statement. Her work is very straightforward and elegantly clean.

Jewelry featuring wire set pearls and twisted wires by Wendy Witchner.

Fine line wire earrings by Wendy Witchner. Even though the picture is arranged in an aesthetically pleasing way, the earrings are to be worn pointing outward.

Bracelets by Wendy Witchner.

Wire as Adornment

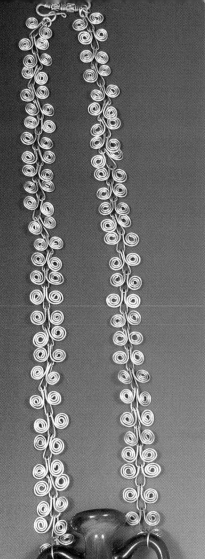

Sterling spiral linked necklace and glass vessel by LeRoy Goertz. Photo by Almac Camera.

LeRoy Goertz

LeRoy Goertz is an inventor. As a boy, his immediate family did not consider or acknowledge art as a profession; in fact it was ridiculed. Like so many of us, he remembers this adult criticism discouraging the creativity that nourishes in children naturally; the art is temporarily posted on the refrigerator and creativity guided towards productivity. For LeRoy, this influence led to furniture building and woodworking. Later, an uncle, who was an art teacher, was making swans out of blown glass. At that time, LeRoy, who was also a teacher, believed he was not an artist, but the glass drew his attention. By the time he was 26, he was helping his uncle at demonstrations and intuitively knew he could work with glass. He quit teaching and opened a small store on the coast of Oregon.

"In terms of creativity, we have ideas in our head. It is specifically those ideas that keep us from being creative," LeRoy reflects. He had always thought to be an artist you had to do something realistic.

A turning point came in the 1970s, during a snowstorm, while on his way to a Las Vegas Christmas show. He saw the abstract work of Jean Paul Legume. With all his glass experience, LeRoy tried it and couldn't do it. He really took a serious look at art. "In every art form there is a language, and you must express yourself in that particular language." Art is serendipitous. Intentional or subliminal, it is a process of constantly correcting mistakes. It is responsive.

In the early '90s, LeRoy started casting bronze. He lost the depth perception in his vision due to an eye disease and began to seriously doubt his artistic career. He picked up wire because he was able

Wire Collar and Bracelet with precious metal caps by LeRoy Goertz. Photo by Almac Camera.

Wire *in* Design

to work with it without depth perception; he had a love-hate relationship with the medium. By chance, he was introduced to the work of an associate, a student of Lynne Merchant (see page 58). He was greatly impacted by the fascinating beads consisting of wire handwork and wanted to invent a way to wrap wire that was faster and could produce long lengths—the result was The Coiling Gizmo. The inspiration came at a time when LeRoy was searching for a direction. "Beethoven had a dry period for five years. All artists need to know that," LeRoy offers.

I asked LeRoy an obvious question, "How many ways can you create jewelry with wrapped wire?" He didn't really answer. He still doesn't consider himself a jewelry designer. He makes jewelry to show the potential of his invention, the potential for design that he has introduced to many artists. His thoughts these days are drifting back to his first love, wood sculpture, and a creative move into music. But how many ways can you design with wrapped wire? I know the answer myself: as many ways as a wave breaks on the shore. LeRoy just makes it faster.

Copper and Forest Green Double Coiled Wire Neckpiece by LeRoy Goertz, with bead by Barbara A. McGuire. Photo by George Post.

Coiled and hammered clasp by LeRoy Goertz.

Inclusive hook and eye by LeRoy Goertz.

■ ■ ■ ■ ■ ■

"In every art form there is a language, and you must express yourself in that particular language."

--LeRoy Goertz

This is a great design using any colored or sterling wire.

■ Materials ■

2 feet 18 gauge colored wire
10 feet 20 gauge silver wire
4 feet 18 gauge silver wire
10" 16 gauge silver wire
The Coiling Gizmo
Chain making pliers
Round nose pliers
Flush cutters
1/4" diameter mandrel

1. Using the 20 gauge wire, make a coil spring with the thin crank rod. Utilize the entire length of the rod. Remove the spring from the winder and snip the wire flush at each end. Insert a core wire into the spring (18 gauge). Make a bead by winding the spring around the thin crank rod (Figure 1). You will need to start a few turns of the core wire first and finish off with a few turns of the core wire also. It also may take a little practice when you first start to wind the spring. Make three beads.

2. To make two coil spring spacer beads from the colored wire, use the 1/4" diameter mandrel (Figure 2). Wrap the wire around the mandrel ten to twelve times. Cut the wire at each end of this spring.

■ ■ ■ ■ ■ ■

Tips:

■ Stretching the wire can make an interesting effect. Try stretching the initial coil spring and threading the core wire through it and then do the second coiling.

■ Stretch the coil spring from the second coiling if you want extra length.

■ You may choose to use more than two beads to create a longer bracelet.

■ Use contrasting colors for the coil spring spacers, the core wire, or the 16 gauge center wire.

Figure 1

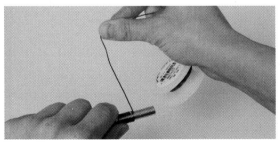

Figure 2

3. To assemble the bracelet, thread these beads onto the 16 gauge wire, alternating with the two coil spacer beads. Make an eye on one end of the wire (Figure 3). Cut the wire at the other end and make a hook (Figure 4).

Figure 3

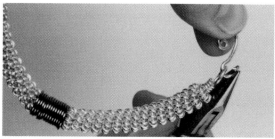

Figure 4

■ ■ ■ ■ ■ ■

Artists have frequently used tools in the creation of art. Tools can be as simple as a cocktail straw, coffee stirrer, Popsicle stick, drill, or a board with nails—or as complex as the deluxe version of a tool that winds extraordinary lengths of wire. The goal is that the artist is aided in the process of creation, and the piece reflects the artist, not the tool.

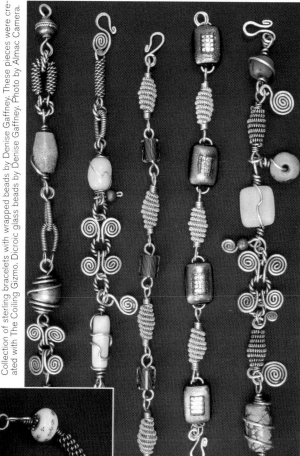

Collection of sterling bracelets with wrapped beads by Denise Gaffney. These pieces were created with The Coiling Gizmo. Dicroic glass beads by Denise Gaffney. Photo by Almac Camera.

Coiled half round sterling bracelets by Denise Gaffney, with glass beads by Lisa Niven. Photo by Almac Camera.

Wire as Adornment

Copper coiled beads with wrapped stone pendants by Corrine Curry. Photo by Almac Camera.

 efore I met Corrine Gurry, I had taken jigs for granted. It seemed like a simple concept: a bunch of pegs in a block. Corrine, however, introduced the jig as the most amazing tool, one of infinite possibilities. She invented a quality jig to perform to her needs and introduced the concept to thousands of artists at conferences, classes, and shows. Currently, Corrine is discovering art clay (silver clay hardened with firing) in combination with wire. It is the constant development that drives her and a reason her jig has been so engaging.

Corrine started her creative career as a silversmith and moved into wire. With wire, she was able to incorporate another interest that she discovered in Hawaii, calligraphy. How do wire and calligraphy relate? Some of the shapes are derived from a letter or a word. One of her favorite links (shown in her project, page 84) is an interpretation of "two women under one roof means trouble." This is reflective of her experience in many Asian cultures where a wife and mother-in-law live in the same house.

One reason for the success of her work is that Corrine thoroughly understands the way wire is hardened, a benefit that makes the wire sturdy as it is designed into a shape or a connecting link. She calls it "work hardening" as a result of an "electron flux charge." When the wire is bent, it creates friction, which carries an electric charge, electron to electron, and this charge flows through the wire. This is the reason a piece of wire can be soft in the middle and hard at the end. The end hardness is a result of the momentum of the transfer of energy or the flow of the charge to the end. A hammered piece also gets hot and work hardens the wire. This is the reason a jigged necklace can be freeform yet sturdy.

Corrine's jig is special because she made it to be handheld. She travels frequently and is able to work on location. The holes accommodate all different peg sizes, but they are slightly smaller at one end, which prevents them from slipping through the jig. You can, however, insert the wire through the jig, which is the way Corrine starts her designs. She leaves an extra length so that the end absorbs the hardening and her design is still workable. Corrine has patented her invention and continues to develop new patterns and designs, as well as video instruction for working with wire.

Each artist has unique personal preferences, and I noticed that Corrine had some favorites when it came to tools. She uses bent nose pliers, which allow her to work from behind a piece and do not obscure her view. Corrine also prefers oval jump rings and has a special tool for nesting the ring and clamping it into a slight oval. Oval rings, Corrine advises, will guarantee that the joint is midway in the oval, so the connection is not working the ring apart. Often, she will make round jump rings double and even triple loops to increase the reliability. This also adds another design element to the piece, the repetition of the lines.

Corrine keeps her mistakes and pins them on a bulletin board with reminders of what went wrong and what to avoid next time. Corrine encourages, "You strive for excellence, not perfection. Perfection is a job. Excellence is a joy. Excellent can always become most excellent."

■　■　■　■　■　■

Tip from Corrine

When finishing a single thickness of wire, Corrine whacks the elements between two steel bench blocks. This hardens and flattens the wire evenly simultaneously. If you have overlapping or crisscrossing wires, it is necessary to sandwich the elements between leather rounds before whacking with the bench blocks. This is to prevent metal fatigue at the cross points, which could make the piece fall apart. She also uses a soft piece of leather folded in half to polish and straighten wire.

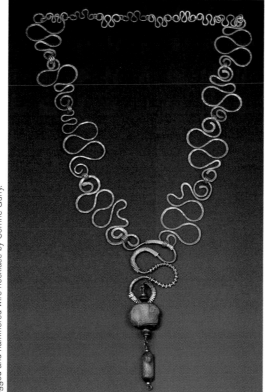

Jigged and hammered wire necklace by Corrine Gurry.

Project from Corrine Gurry:
Two Women Under One Roof

■ Materials ■

Flush cutters
Round nose pliers
Chain nose pliers
Bent nose pliers
Loop closer pliers
Ball pein hammer
18 gauge silver, gold, gold-filled, or
   jeweler's brass wire
Bench blocks, 4" square and 2-3/4" square
Two pieces of leather
Wire Wizard (jig)

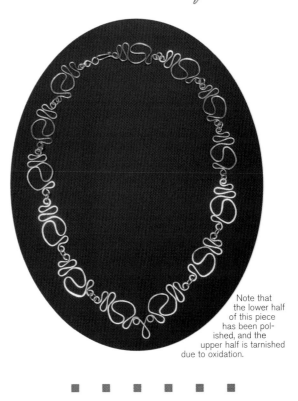

Note that the lower half of this piece has been polished, and the upper half is tarnished due to oxidation.

1. Cut twelve pieces of 18 gauge wire to 1 foot lengths (ten for links, one for the clasp, and one for the jump rings). Cut one piece of 18 gauge wire to 18" long (for the yoke).

2. Place the pegs on the Wire Wizard jig according to the pattern (Figure 1). Take a 1-foot long piece of wire and poke an inch of it in the hole next to the beginning peg. Bend the wire down to the surface of the jig and begin wrapping wire around the pegs as shown (Figure 2).

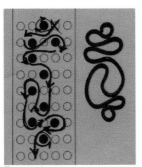

Figure 1

3. Following the peg pattern, bend the wire. Don't tug the wire too tight; try to keep the curves a bit more voluptuous, then tighten up the tension to finish. The consistency of tension is what gives you close reproductions of each pattern.

4. Trim the excess wire ends at the top and bottom; use round nose pliers to close the loops (Figure 3). Using your fingers, close gaps in the element.

■ ■ ■ ■ ■ ■

Just a slight variation in the direction of the peg, or a variation in the overlap, will result in a completely different centerpiece. To make matching parts, or a balanced headpiece, the work is removed while it is still in process and flipped to wind the continuing symmetry. The finishing clasps are designed to be either accentuated or blend in.

5. Place the element on a square bench block. Then, holding the other bench block in your hand, smack straight down (you become the hammer) with three quick strikes (Figure 4); your element will be flat on both sides. Now you can texturize the wire with the ball pein hammer.

6. To make the yoke of the necklace, repeat the peg pattern in mirror image and begin jigging in the middle, working toward the outer pegs (Figure 5).

7. By adding an extra peg at either end of the link element pattern and winding wire up, over, and back down, you can turn the "hook" sideways to make the clasp. Hammer between two pieces of leather to harden, then twist the hook just formed so it stands up. Now you have a matching clasp for your necklace.

8. Using a 1/8"-diameter knitting needle, take 1 foot of wire and wrap as to cover the nee-dle until you run out of wire. Use the flush cutters to cut off the excess. Cut the rings, one at a time, making the second cut immediately behind the first.

9. A bevel will be left on the coil when you cut off the jump ring. Turn the cutter over and nip off the little shiny beveled bit, giving a flush cut to start the next jump ring. Make two cuts per jump ring. Using notched loop closer pliers, putting the opening in the jump ring into the top notch of the pliers, squeeze gently to close the jump ring. With a bit more pressure, the jump ring will be a little oval (Figure 6). (An oval jump ring is strong and allows gravity to keep an element from resting in the opening. Hammering the jump rings between bench blocks makes them even stronger.)

10. Now you are ready to assemble the elements to create a lovely, handcrafted piece of jewelry (Figure 7).

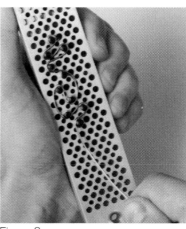
Figure 2

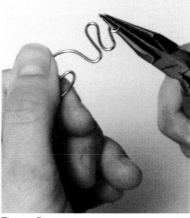
Figure 3

Figure 4

Figure 5

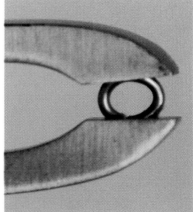
Figure 6

Figure 7

Chapter 6

WIRE AS DECORATION AND IMAGINATION

Joy Boy Clock by Marvin and Michelle Shafer of Q3 Art. Photo by Larry Sanders.

Wire With Intention

The artists in this group have created art with purpose. The wire and the art are intended to be useful, *for use*. Most of the historical wire art was functional, and these artists have carried that tradition but have taken it to a new level. They have surpassed the mundane utilitarian function and turned homes into galleries where art can live as well as serve. Once you are introduced to the service of wire, you will consider it your favorite creative tool, and you can create anything you want.

Demitasse spoons by Ellen Wieske.

Wire That Makes You Smile

I suppose you could create a great big smile with a piece of wire and hang it on your wall. That's the essence of what these artists have done: the wire makes you smile. Maybe because a cascade of curls looks like a giggle, or maybe because the hair on a doll looks like *your* hair. Whatever the expression, this wire is charming, delightful, and fun. It is filled with imagination and dares to be eccentric. When you want to break the mold, grab your wire and do something outrageous!

Springtime Clock by Marvin and Michelle Shafer of 3Q Art. Photo by Larry Sanders.

Cup with handle by Ellen Wieske.

Mediterranean furniture set by Julianna Hudgins. Photo by Graig Cook.

Wire as Decoration and Imagination

Distinctive Designs

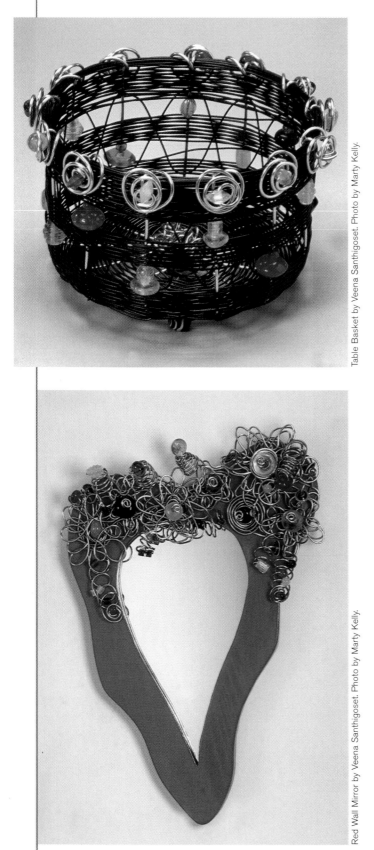

Table Basket by Veena Santhigoset. Photo by Marty Kelly.

Red Wall Mirror by Veena Santhigoset. Photo by Marty Kelly.

*T*o get to Veena Santhigoset's studio, I needed to walk through a Thai restaurant in the Mission district of San Francisco. I was tempted to stop for lunch, but I was too excited because I was about to meet the artist who creates the bold spiral decorated baskets I have begun to collect. Veena and her husband own and operate Distinctive, a studio that produces basket-like containers, frames, and many other decorative items for the home such as clocks, candlesticks, wine holders, pencil holders, and vases. These creations are hand fashioned from heavy copper, aluminum, and coated black wire. They are massive and abound with colorful glass and clay beads. Distinctive's designs are easily recognized, repeating the theme of the spiral and primary colors in the majority of the work.

I asked Veena how it all began, and she said one day her friend, an architect, gave her wire and pliers and encouraged to just have some fun. She sat on the floor and worked the wire into a basket. She was delighted with her new creation and was hooked on wire. Her background as a fashion designer gave her the encouragement to discover and go with her instincts. She purchased tie wire from a hardware store and began practicing, weaving while sitting on the floor, creating baskets in different sizes.

At that time, her husband was running a business that offered hand-painted linens. At a January gift show, he displayed five of Veena's baskets, all of which sold. They began taking orders for more, increasing their business five-fold. Production started in their home and later moved to a location where the huge inventory is in constant rotation.

Originally, the wire used was black and had to constantly be wiped and sprayed with a protective sealant. Now, Veena has discovered a new coated wire and also frequently uses copper or aluminum. She makes four to six new designs every six months for shows. She makes some just for herself, and everything else is made to order. She's never taken classes, and her designs evolve from her curiosity, playfulness, and personal character to constantly be producing. She prefers to stay at home and work together with the loyal employees she has had for nearly five years. Veena's designs illustrate how the age-old tradition of basket weaving together with modern wire materials can evolve into a beautiful hand craft.

■　■　■　■　■　■

Distinctive's designs are easily recognized, repeating the theme of the spiral and primary colors in the majority of the work.

Clock by Veena Santhigoset. Photo by Marty Kelly.

Floor Basket by Veena Santhigoset. Photo by Marty Kelly.

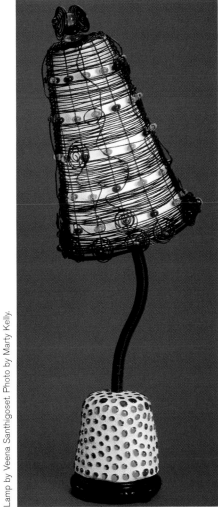

Lamp by Veena Santhigoset. Photo by Marty Kelly.

Copper Box by Veena Santhigoset. Photo by Marty Kelly.

Ackfeld Mfg.

*S*ince 1984, Edward Ackfeld, of Ackfeld Mfg., has been producing commercial wire products—including garden art—by hand. This is reminiscent of the factories around the turn of the twentieth century that produced the wire objects found in catalogs and hardware stores. This company also caters to a small niche of craft design customers who want to design their own products and have them commercially made. The amazing thing is that Ackfeld Mfg. can compete with overseas prices and produce quality results.

The wire Edward Ackfeld uses arrives in a 4,000 lb. spool. Most of the wire is coated or electroplated to keep costs low. The wire also comes in four different tensile strengths, and the design dictates which wire is best suited for a project. The process begins with the customer's design and dimensions, then a bid is entered, a purchase order submitted, and a sample produced. Finally, production begins. The designs are shaped with jigs.

The commercial items Ackfeld produces still retain a charming hand-made appeal. The designs are visually balanced and utilize space very effectively. The sequences in the hooks and shapes also create pattern and rhythm. Essentially, the wire is a contour drawing of familiar folk art themes. The simple country designs make a functional item uncommonly delightful. In short, Ackfeld Mfg. continues the tradition of tinkering in modern times.

■　■　■　■　■　■

The designs are visually balanced and utilize space very effectively. The sequences in the hooks and shapes also create pattern and rhythm.

Dancing Bubbles

$\mathcal{D}$avid Strongheart and his wife, Terri Smith, of Dancing Bubbles, fell into making bubble wands as scavengers of a magical experience, gaining inspiration from the moment. It was even magical that I found their wands in a remote community, in a tiny candy store, on the coast of California.

On many occasions, the two traveled on a bubble and a prayer. It was a blessing that got them through the Oklahoma City bombing in 1995. They arrived in town with only enough money to do the county fair. The circumstance of the bomb left them without a fair and without gas money to leave town. David insisted that Terri had to blow bubbles and sell the wands to survive. Courage persisted, and the couple ended up in a "red brick town" where people bought the bubble wands. The couple traveled

on, and their luck continued as the wands grew popular at state fairs—people were captivated with the delight of the activity.

Terri's wire bubble wands all come with a recipe for creating your own bubbles. The rainbow handle is captured by a wire twirl and capped with a glass marble. Bubbles have streamed from wands that link, wands that twirl, and wands that are simply delightful sculpture.

Terri is constantly grateful for her fortunes and shares, "It's not about the work; there is a piece of each person in the wand. The fairy element drives on. The essence is what you want."

■   ■   ■   ■   ■

On many occasions, the couple traveled on a bubble and a prayer.

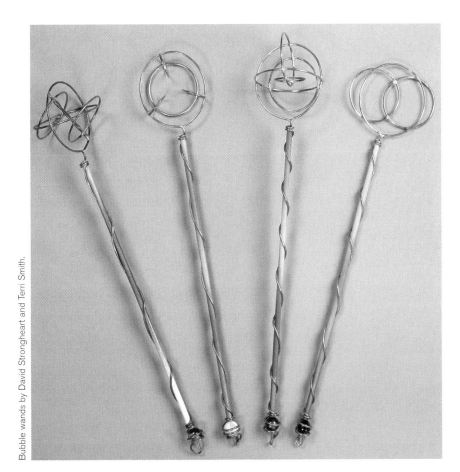

Bubble wands by David Strongheart and Terri Smith.

Wire as Decoration and Imagination

Bob Calton

Blue Moon by Bob Calton. Photo by Adam Geiss.

Custom lamp by Bob Calton. Photo by Adam Geiss.

The human being is continuously drawn to faces. Interaction is a means of survival. It is no wonder that Bob Calton is fascinated with the image of a face. Even a small variation produces a different personality and illustrates a different attitude. The illumination of the glass provides a "living" energy, a depth of light value. The large, open spatial areas of the glass form and the spindly legs balance the details in the wire features. The face is actually a contour line drawing done in wire.

Bob has been told by admirers that his craft is reminiscent of Alexander Calder's wirework (see page 39); however, he was never exposed to Calder's wire portraits and discovered the effects entirely on his own. Many discoveries happen to artists independently, although people may assume that the idea was transferred from one artist to another. This should not discourage an artist from continuing a style or developing a design; a personal expression will emerge regardless of whether it is similar to another's expression. A spiral or a spring is not "owned" by any artist; any one person was not the "first" to discover it. A spiral can be seen for years before a person actually "discovers" it. It's the same with a face. A theme becomes personal when an artist embraces it. A personal style becomes more obvious when you see an entire collection of work from a particular artist. Continuity evolves and you can see the relationship between the pieces, even in something as simple as the way the beads are consistently arranged. This is an example of taking an element of the design that you like and are comfortable with, and keeping that element intact while expanding on other elements. Bob's pieces are wonderfully individual, but you can see that they are all related. His characters have become his friends, and this is Bob's personal account of how that came to be:

"I became interested in twig furniture in '93

and made a number of pieces, one of which included a little lamp. I enjoyed the lamp so much that I created several more. Then, one day, some wire I was messing with was formed into a face. When I soldered it on a lamp, it spoke to me! All of my current work are characters of some sort, and I believe they speak well of me."

■   ■   ■   ■   ■   ■

Bob has been told by admirers that his craft is reminiscent of Alexander Calder's wirework; however, he was never exposed to Calder's wire portraits and discovered the effects entirely on his own.

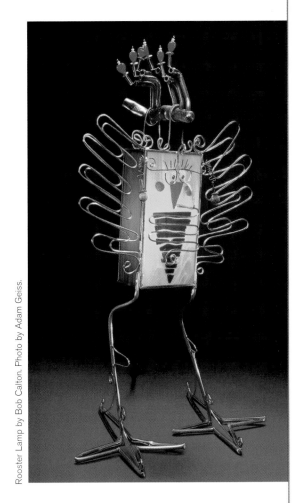

Rooster Lamp by Bob Calton. Photo by Adam Geiss.

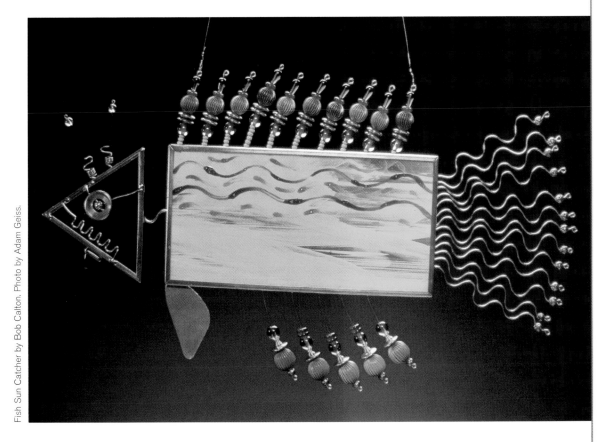

Fish Sun Catcher by Bob Calton. Photo by Adam Geiss.

Wire as Decoration and Imagination

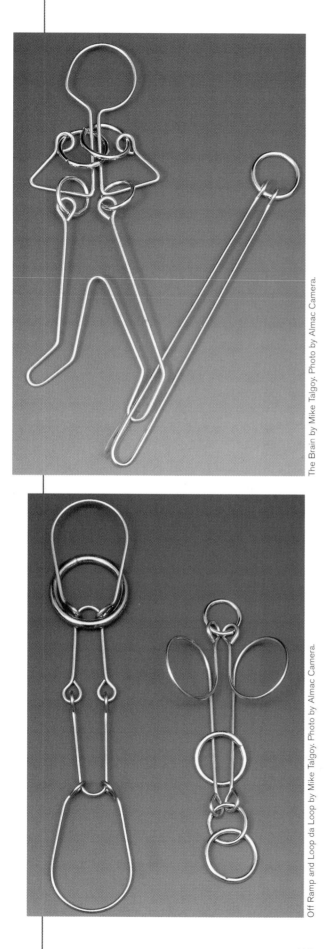

The Brain by Mike Talgoy. Photo by Almac Camera.

Off Ramp and Loop da Loop by Mike Talgoy. Photo by Almac Camera.

Some people have a knack for figuring things out—and Mike Talgoy of WireWorks Puzzles is one of them. His skills excel to the capacity of being a scientist, and for many years he worked in Winnipeg on cancer research, utilizing a masters degree in Biochemistry. How does a research scientist begin inventing puzzles? Like many inquisitive minds, he became interested in puzzles. He came across a book by Jerry Slocum on how to make and solve puzzles. One section was a series of wire puzzles, disentanglement puzzles. This captured Mike's attention.

Mike made his first puzzles out of coat hangers and brought them to the lab. His colleagues flipped out over the toys and played with them during lunch. Requests followed for Mike to make some for their friends. Everyone was fighting over the puzzles! Mike then started offering them at craft shows, in addition to performing his research. People bought the puzzles, and after the second year, Mike was making as much money making puzzles as doing research (research is not a particularly lucrative field). He had been doing lab work for twelve years and he decided to try being his own boss and inventor; Mike has spent the past eleven years making puzzles.

The puzzles are made of 1/8-inch and 3/32-inch welding rod that has been copper-coated. The wire arrives in a 50 lb. box of straightened wire. Some of the wire is nickel-plated. The company that supplies Mike's wire straightens and cuts it if he wants. The particular type of wire Mike uses accommodates bending by hand. He uses a jig to produce uniformity and duplicate the designs. The curve in the design is created from using different sized bolts. Some of the rings, such as the nickel pieces, are purchased.

Mike has no formal art training. His wife, Mary Sauder, helps sketch and draw the designs, and she asks Michael to work out the puzzle. They hand the project back and forth many times before production begins. Production is much of the consideration in the final design. "A lot of the design is symmetrical because it looks good," Mike says about his artistic intention. This is a good example of the elements and principles at work in an instinctive sense. The proportion and duplication of the bends produce rhythm. The lines lead the eye through the pieces and produce shapes that are very pleasing and recognizable.

To introduce a design, Mike and Mary give it to fifteen of their friends and acquaintances and ask for opinions and how difficult the puzzle is to solve. They found customers preferred a color difference in the wire, which supports the design principle that contrast creates interest. The copper wire will eventually tarnish when oxygen in the air reacts with it. This creates value, or a range of color from light to dark within a certain hue (copper). Customers do not complain—and they can always keep the item in a plastic bag to limit tarnishing.

Mike and Mary come out with several new puzzle designs each year, designed for all ages. I have yet to solve one. It's not that they are that difficult; I just view them as incredible works of art that I want to keep in one piece.

■   ■   ■   ■   ■

Mike has no formal art training. His wife, Mary Sauder, helps sketch and draw the designs, and she asks Michael to work out the puzzle.

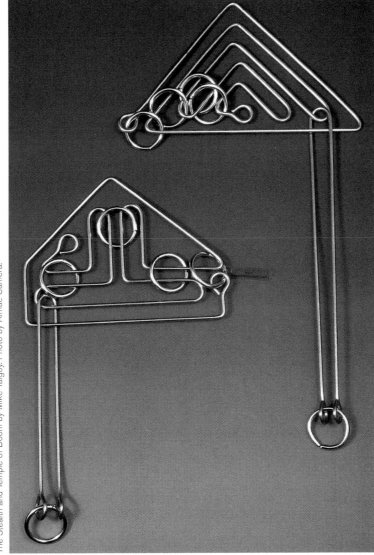

The Stealth and Temple of Doom by Mike Talgoy. Photo by Almac Camera.

Wire as Decoration and Imagination

Moonbabies

Moonbabies are little dolls on a stick. In fact, the stickpin with the "kinked hair" is the signature piece to this trademark.

Moonbabies came about during a blizzard when designer Ava Minsky Foxman wanted a way to entertain her children and their friends who were snowed in. She designed the little wire people to look like each of the six children. "When working with children on craft or science projects," Ava says, "I find the wire useful and easy in connecting the parts." The dolls have distinct personalities—there are more than 300 characters in all. Because of the flexibility of the wire, it enables Ava to pose the pieces, which also adds to the expression.

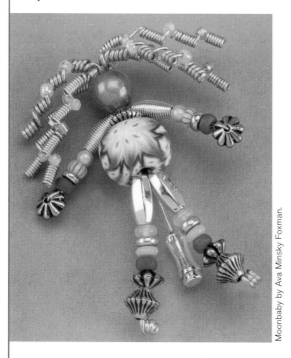

Moonbaby by Ava Minsky Foxman.

She had always wanted to do something philanthropic and creative in a career, thus Moonbabies—named after her birth sign, Cancer, known as moon children—where born, blending the two desires together. Over 100,000 Moonbabies have been sold, many of which were assembled by moms in their homes. The dolls have style and heart. The components range from plastic to diachronic glass and have evolved into stickpins, earrings, badge holders, and key rings. Ten percent of each Moonbabies sale goes to the Elizabeth Glazer Pediatric AIDS foundation.

Ava is a graduate of the Fashion Institute in California and worked as a clothing designer for several years. Now she dresses her wire dolls. How many ways can you dress a wire doll? Well, in a woman's world, the answer is infinitely infinite. How many ways can you design a wire doll? That's infinite, too. Many artists have designed dolls. A face and a doll are immediately familiar forms. As humans, the face and figure are two of the first images we recognize—for survival. How can such universal images be unique, especially when people use the same medium? The uniqueness comes from the personal expression of a unique individual. You will see continuity in a person's work when it is truly expressive of themselves. All the influences of a lifetime are built into the preferences of a person's creativity. A common theme, such as a wire doll, is not a limitation to be creative but an invitation to offer a new perspective on something that has proven popular throughout time.

■　■　■　■　■　■

Over 100,000 Moonbabies have been sold, and many of them are assembled by moms in their homes... Ten percent of each Moonbabies sale goes to the Elizabeth Glazer Pediatric AIDS foundation.

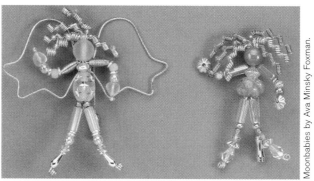

Moonbabies by Ava Minsky Foxman.

■ ■ ■ ■ ■

Dolls, like masks, are a universal and appealing object for artists to create in expressing their imagination. Wire lends itself to embellishment, as well as being a structural component in the creation of dolls. The curly spirals are a common theme for a doll's "good hair day."

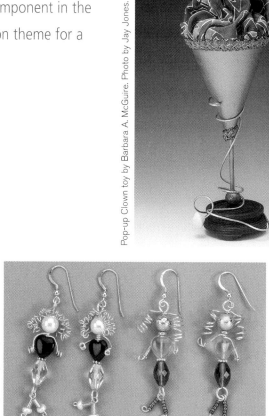

Pop-up Clown toy by Barbara A. McGuire. Photo by Jay Jones.

The Girls by Margaret Kristof. Photo by Jay Jones.

Earring dolls by Cathy Ames.

Polymer Clay and Wire Doll by Anne Lou Robkin.

Flower Heads by Veena Santhigoset of Distinctive Designs. Photo by Mark Boscacci.

Wire as Decoration and Imagination

Wild Hair Day by Chris Gluck. Photo by Lori Landalle.

Mobile form by Chris Gluck.

Chris Gluck

hris Gluck had the extraordinary experience of creating a wire project with 700 people in one day. The occasion was Ben & Jerry's One World One People celebration in Vermont. This was a clue to Chris that perhaps there was a broad audience that would enjoy creating art with wire. Chris' introduction to wire began much earlier; when she was a child, she found scraps of telephone wire workmen would leave behind on the street. The treasures—filled with bends and twists—were colorful, tactile, responsive, and fascinating. "It makes you think. It makes you play," Chris explains.

Chris rekindled her fascination with wire years later with her own children, and she started to make arts and crafts projects with kids during a two-hour after-school program she established in her home in 1994. Chris discovered a source from the phone company, and the design in wire became more method oriented. The coils became beads. Combined with wood and glass beads, the look was complete. The program was 100-percent educational, focusing on the development of small motor skills. Wire is easier to bead than a string, so success, satisfaction, and esteem levels are guaranteed in the projects. The poly-coated wire also is more forgiving, hiding crimps and unwanted kinks. The method was so efficient she could teach forty children in one class! As her ideas developed, the coils were wrapped around varying forms, including straws, craft sticks, and stirrers, that altered the design form of the bead. From a simple coil, Chris varied texture and movement to include twists, crimps, and loops in one bead form.

Chris discovered she could package any given project and achieve the desired results with simple instructions and the merits of the contents. The original wire kits in plastic bags she developed for the One World celebration had both adults and children completely mesmerized. That's when Chris' entrepreneurial spirit generated her company, Wire Art. The results were an assortment of stylish kits that were able to communicate the fun packaged inside. She marketed Wire Art kits for retail sale in 1997 and drew attention to a style of design in wire that is popular today.

Chris believes wire is here to stay. It is an art medium that has as much expression as paint, crayon, or clay. She also feels wire is an exceptional medium to teach sculpture. Her newest creations are simple wire sculptures, incorporating lots of space, something she has made in tribute to the inspiration of Alexander Calder (see page 39). Like Calder, the movement illustrated in the wire defies gravity and becomes a playful circus of line and rhythm.

■   ■   ■   ■   ■   ■

Chris discovered she could package any given project and achieve the desired results with simple instructions and the merits of the contents... That's when Chris' entrepreneurial spirit generated her company, Wire Art.

Wire as Decoration and Imagination

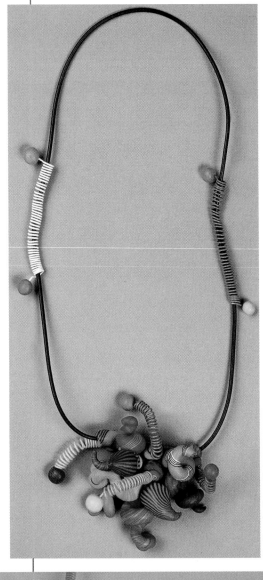

Necklace by Donna Kato.

Colorful poly-coated wire makes an excellent medium for festive jewelry. The wiggles and bouncy coils add playfulness to designs.

Bangle bracelets by P.K. Hille-Hatten. Photo by Almac Camera.

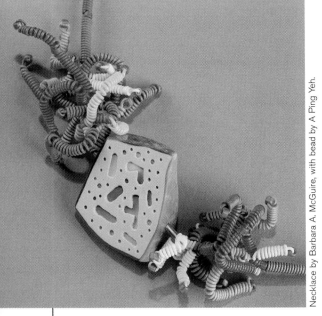

Necklace by Barbara A. McGuire, with bead by A Ping Yeh.

Clay and wire dolls by Susie R. Bingham.

Face Bracelet by Robert P. McGuire.

Wire *in* Design

Kathy Peterson

If you have seen someone doing a wire project on TV or in a magazine, chances are it was Kathy Peterson. Kathy has also written books, hosted how-to videos, and is a columnist for national craft magazines. How did wire catch Kathy's eye? Like many artists, it began with a challenge. She says, "In 1998, I received a bag of broken stained glass, so I wrapped it with wire. I had to solve the problem of 'what the heck to do with all the broken stained glass,' and rather than do mosaics, which was a simple solution, I expanded my imagination with wire. Six months later I had my first wire book."

It's a given that anyone who likes to "produce," including TV production, would be drawn to a medium that is multi-faceted. Wire adapted itself to all of the other media Kathy was familiar with, such as wood, beads, glass, paper, clay, leather, textiles, and buttons. Many of her pieces reflect a playful freedom and inventive combination of materials. Her work utilizes wire as a line element in the total composition. And the spiral is a popular form that she uses for pattern, rhythm, and balance. But the appeal in Kathy's design is the whimsical personality of each piece. I will venture to guess that out of the 300 projects Kathy has designed over the last two years, each one wears a smile.

Wire wall doll by Kathy Peterson.

■　■　■　■　■　■

Many of Kathy's pieces reflect a playful freedom and inventive combination of materials.

Fairy Wand by Randy Neu.

Wire helps to create functional objects with flair. You can create decorative items throughout the home with wire mirrors, baskets, candleholders, and vases. These items need not always be functional, but are pleasurable in their aesthetic quality alone.

Basket by Bev Morgan.

Candle votives and hanging flower vase by Randy Neu.

Frame by Bev Morgan.

Chopsticks by Diane Cook.

Frame by Desiree McCrorey. Photo by Desiree McCrorey.

Wire *in* Design

PART IV

PUTTING

IT

ALL

TOGETHER

Chapter 7

PROJECTS

After you've become inspired from all of the artists in the book, you are probably anticipating some projects. Those presented here are geared toward tapping into your own personal interpretation, application, and direction in wire. They represent everything from sculpture to embellishment. Many are mixed media projects because it is stimulating to experiment with new and different products. There is a wide range of gauges and colors and a complete variety of techniques, including wrapping, weaving, coiling, linking, bending, and balancing—not to mention jigging!

While you are designing, expect to make a few "mistakes," which can be good—rarely does anyone just sit down and create a perfect piece. The design evolves, and one thing leads to another. A change in color can dictate a complete change in the mood of a piece. Artists change their minds, they run out of materials, they adapt, they improvise, they substitute, they practice, they explore. And they have a lot of fun doing it. Be bold, be free, and don't hold back in the essence of your creativity.

Note: See the basic techniques on pages 24 to 28 for creating spirals, wrapping, jump rings, and eye pins.

Basic Instructions for Polymer Clay

Polymer clay is an extremely useful medium for artistic creativity, and many of the projects in Chapter 7 incorporate clay in the design. For those unfamiliar with polymer clay, the following are basic instructions that will help you get started.

Polymer clay is essentially Polyvinyl Chloride (PVC) and is available in many colors, in small or large packages; you can purchase it through the Internet or in craft stores. The popular brand names are FIMO, FIMO Soft, Sculpey, Premo, and Cernit. Each varies somewhat in softness before curing and durability after curing.

Common tools used with polymer clay are an acrylic brayer or roller, an extremely sharp polymer clay blade, a pasta machine (dedicated to clay usage), card stock used as a working and baking surface, and an oven.

All polymer clay must be conditioned before use. This is a process of kneading the clay until it is pliable and the molecules have been aligned, ready for the clay to stretch. This is most frequently done with a pasta machine, but you can also use your hands. Chop the clay into small pieces or slice it into thin slabs. Use a small food processor (dedicated to clay) if the clay is firm. Form the clay into a thin pancake and run it through the pasta machine, doubling it onto itself and running it through again until it is pliable.

Once you have utilized the clay in whatever art you are creating, it must be cured to become permanent. Curing is done by baking the clay. Many artists have a small portable oven designated to clay use, but it can be done in a home oven (do not bake food at the same time!). The manufacturer will provide specific instructions for baking the clay, which makes it hard; however, most clays cure when baked at 265° to 275° F for 20 to 30 minutes. You may have to bake the piece longer if it is thick. The clay hardens as it cools, and it does not shrink during baking. It can be drilled, painted, sanded, and polished or varnished as the work requires. Store unused clay in an airtight container, away from heat and light.

Project 1

Project 3

Project 5

Project 6

Project 8

Project 7

Project 11

Project 12

Wired Label

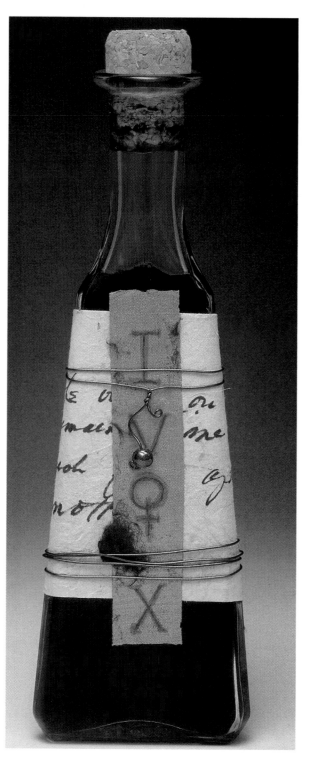

In olden days, wire was used to mend broken pottery and bottles. This application of wire holding a label of a bottle reminds me of the days before we had glues and tapes. The wire provides a line element to divide the spatial relations in the design. The two wire wraps are balanced. The green shiny wire contrasts with the matte finish of the paper. The wire is wrapped several times to create impact and draw emphasis to the space between the wraps, namely the label.

■ Materials ■

Bottle (triangular is shown)
Handmade paper, beige and gold
Brown marker
Two lengths of 20 gauge wire from Artistic Wire, green
Optional: Miscellaneous beads

1. Cut a rectangular piece of beige paper to wrap around the bottle, with a 1" overlap. (In the sample, there was an angle cut in one of the rectangle's ends so that the edge was vertical when the paper was wrapped around the bottle, because the bottle is a triangular form. The shape of your paper will depend on your bottle.)

2. Write a favorite verse on the paper with the brown marker (Figure 1).

3. Wrap the bottle, overlapping the paper in the back; the verse should be exposed (Figure 2).

4. Hold the paper and wire and tie the wire as if you are wrapping a present (Figure 3). You can add a few beads to the wire, if desired. The bottom wire is tied at the back of the bottle.

5. Cut a strip of gold paper and draw some letters, numbers, or symbols (the ones shown are completely fictional).

6. Slip the strip into behind the wire. Tighten the wire with a twist (Figure 4).

Figure 1

Figure 2

Figure 3

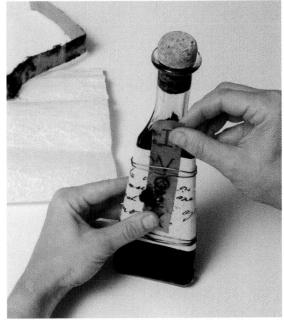

Figure 4

Wire Card

$\mathscr{H}$ere, repeating the same motif in a diminishing size gives rhythm to the design. The boughs are alternated to give the design a pattern of every-other. The wire itself creates texture, and the lines create movement, leading the eye back and forth and to the top. The top spiral is turned upward in contrast to the others, defining that it is the top of the tree. The tree is made of one color to give it unity.

■ Materials ■

2 ft. of 18 gauge PVC-coated wire, purple (Fun Wire was used)

Low-temp hot glue gun and glue stick in sparkle gold

Blank white greeting card

Flush cutters

1. Make several loose spirals (Figures 1 and 2), cutting the finish with a blunt end (Figure 3).

2. The tail of each spiral should curve in a similar manner and diminish in size. These can also be cut when the boughs are fit into the design.

3. Arrange the spirals on the blank card placed above each other, starting with the longest at the bottom. Alternate the direction of the spiral and stagger the pieces to make a tree shape (Figure 4).

4. Turn the last spiral upward to make the top. Align two pieces to make a trunk. These should be shorter and tighter spirals than the others.

5. Once the spirals are lined up, tack each to the paper with a dot of hot glue (Figure 5). Lift the gun upwards and twirl the stringy tails of the glue as you proceed to the next bough (this may take a little practice).

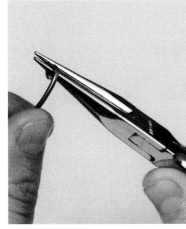

Figure 1

Figure 2

Figure 3

Figure 4

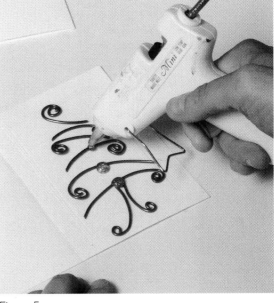

Figure 5

Coiled Colors Necklace

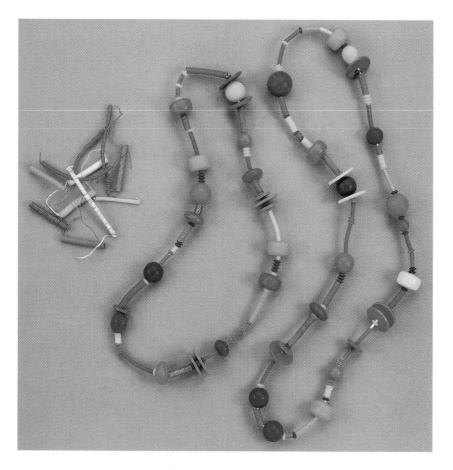

$\mathcal{T}$his necklace is an easy project, but to make it really appealing, there are subtle applications of the elements and principles of design at work. The colors should all have unity (bright, pure colors, not mixed with earth tones). The beads should all be of the same material, either plastic or glass, but consistent enough to have unity in the composition (for instance, one wood bead would create an unpleasant contrast). The contrast is in the placement of the different bead forms. The piece has rhythm but variation to make it exciting. The different beads or bead groupings balance out the visual weight of each cluster. The wrapping provides texture. It has natural movement because the entire piece connects in a circle or oval.

■ Materials ■

2-ft. lengths of 24 gauge telephone or plastic-coated
    wire
The Coiling Gizmo or mandrel (in two sizes)
Assorted beads
18" to 24" of elastic cord for stringing*
Flush cutters
Optional: bead board or piece of cloth with a texture
*The length of the necklace will depend on your preference.

1. Use the coiling gizmo or mandrels to wrap dozens of lengths of telephone wire (Figure 1).

2. Snip the ends in a blunt cut, flush with the coil (Figure 2)

3. Split the coils into varying lengths (Figure 3).

4. Arrange the necklace on a bead board or a piece of cloth with a texture to prevent the beads from rolling around. You can create sections of the composition or the complete necklace (Figure 4).

5. String the beads with elastic. Knot and cut the ends. Tuck the ends into a bead or coil.

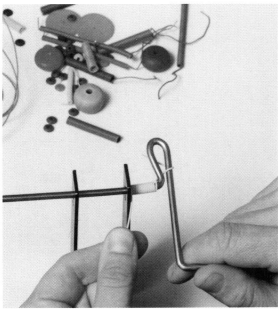

Figure 1

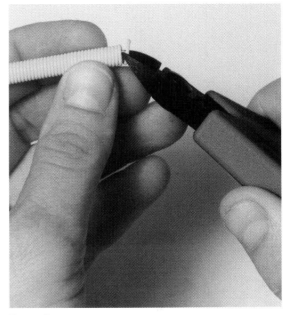

Figure 2

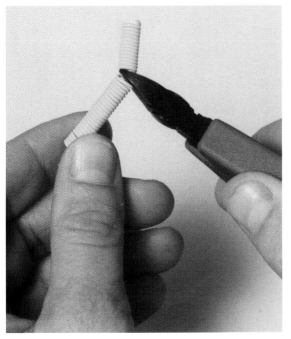

Figure 3

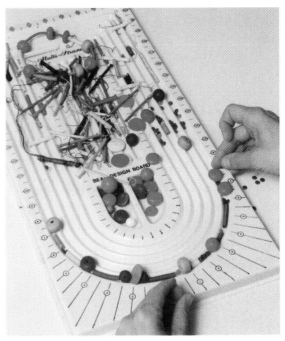

Figure 4

Picture Frame

The future artists of the
Tule Elk Art Studio
wish to acknowledge and thank
the heart and hard work of
Americorps Volunteers:
Melissa Castleberry
And
Danielle Reed
and express gratitude for the
San Francisco Education Fund Grant
October 2000

This is a super project for beginners and can evolve into any kind of patterned frame. It took some time to balance this composition because the movement of the wire leads the eye around the frame, and the visual weight of the pieces varies. In this sample, the inscription is to commemorate services donated to a school. Be sure to invert the type on a computer or a copier so the readability transfers; many copiers offer a "mirror" image.

Note: Use the glass panel in the frame as the base for the project and bake the piece directly on the glass. This helps keep the base flat and stationary as your work. The glass can be set on a piece of card stock when it is put in the oven. The low temperatures will not harm glass or card stock.

■ Materials ■

Photocopy (graphite-based toner) or written commemoration (reversed type), trimmed to size
Rubbing alcohol and cotton swab
FIMO Soft polymer clay, green #505 and blue pastel #305, mixed, and black metallic #912
Acrylic brayer or pasta machine and blade
Crafter's Pick Ultimate Tacky Glue
6" to 18" lengths of PVC-compatible wire in assorted colors (Fun Wire was used)
Whack-It-Down
Mandrel or coiling gizmo
Flush cutters
Round nose pliers
8" x 10" frame and glass panel

1. Completely cover the glass with a large, flat sheet of conditioned black clay, approximately 3/16" thickness. Set aside

2. Combine the blue and green clay to make a designer color; this conditions the clay at the same time as you are mixing the color.

3. Roll the pastel clay (with the acrylic brayer or pasta machine) into a thin sheet, large enough to accommodate the inscription. Place the photocopy on the clay, dip the cotton swab in alcohol, and dampen the back of the photocopy (this helps to release the toner from the paper and transfer it to the clay) (Figure 1). Make sure there are no air bubbles between the paper and the clay.

4. Bake the inscription only (not the frame) according to the manufacturer's instructions (or at 265° for 20 minutes) and allow the clay to cool. If the photocopy doesn't transfer well, you can repeat Step 3 before you have finished the entire project. Pull the paper gently from the clay (Figure 2). If the paper sticks, you can soak it in water and rub it off the clay. Trim the baked clay 1/2" from the edge of the inscription (Figure 3).

5. Coat the back of the baked inscription with Crafter's Pick glue using a cotton swab or your fingers (Figure 4). Place the inscription in the middle of the "frame" and press gently to secure into place.

6. Make several designs with the wire by using the pliers and forming the shapes in your hands (Figure 5). Vary the sizes of spirals, loops, and wiggles—this is really a chance to be inventive and playful.

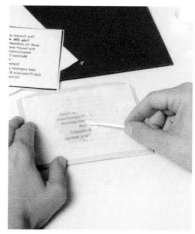

Figure 1

Figure 2

Figure 3

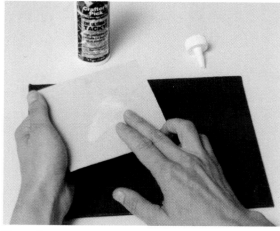

Figure 4

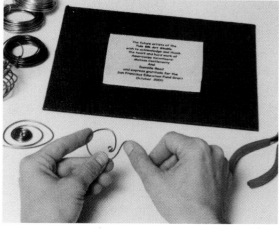

Figure 5

7. Once the shapes are made, you will need to flatten them before placing them on the frame. (I used a product called the Whack-It-Down to flatten and strengthen the wire. I pounded it between two flat, strong, non-abrasive surfaces (Figure 6). Remember the wire is work-hardened by movement and friction.) Set the shapes aside.

8. Make four lengths of wire coil using a mandrel or Coiling Gizmo (Figure 7). Because this is plastic wire, it may stick when you want to release if from the mandrel. Loosen the coils by untwisting them in the opposite direction (Figure 8). Once removed from the mandrel, spread the lengths apart to create a variation in

the tightness of the coil at desired intervals. Press the coils to border the inscription and trim to fit (Figure 9).

9. Place the shapes on the clay "frame" (Figure 10). Don't press them in until you have balanced the entire arrangement. Start with large designs first, then progress to smaller units. Securely press the wire into the clay.

10. Bake the clay and wire together at 265° for 20 minutes, or as the manufacturer directs.

11. Remove from glass. Frame or put on easel.

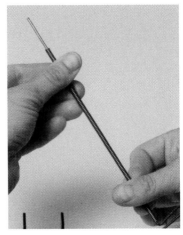

Figure 6

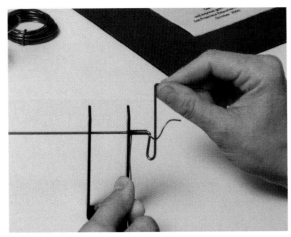

Figure 7

Figure 8

Figure 9

Figure 10

Long Shaped Heart

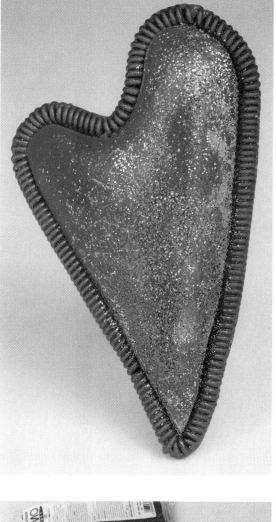

*T*he shape of the heart is timeless, but an elongated shape often adds loftiness, sophistication, and style. Even the slightest variation in the shape will add a different personality to the heart because it is so familiar and recognizable. Using wire spring coils as the border to the heart is a nice finish. You can stretch the springs to vary the rhythm in the coil and add movement around the border.

■ Materials ■

FIMO Soft polymer clay, blue metallic #302
Acrylic brayer or pasta machine
2 to 3 ft. of 24 gauge PVC-coated wire, purple (Fun Wire was used)
Coiling gizmo or mandrel
Flush cutters
Oven
Optional: Sparkling embossing powder
X-acto knife
Pin back

1. With the acrylic brayer or pasta machine, condition and roll a sheet of blue metallic clay, approximately 1/8" thick.

2. Coil the purple wire. **Note:** Because it is plastic-coated, you may have trouble slipping it off the mandrel. If this is the case, unwind the coil in the opposite direction to loosen it.

3. Clip the ends, leaving a 1/2" length, and connect them by straightening and twisting the wires together to hold the ends in place. Tuck both ends into one of the coils (Figure 1).

Figure 1

4. Shape the wire into a heart, in the air, free-forming the shape with your fingers (Figure 2).

5. Stretch the wire and elongate the heart until you have the desired shape. Progress slowly, continuing to shape with your fingers. Pinch the point.

6. Press the shape onto the surface of the sheet of clay.

7. Using the X-acto knife, slice the back edge at an angle through the clay along the wire outline (Figure 3).

8. Once the heart is cut out, smooth the edges and form the shape into a slight curve (Figure 4). This adds interest to the form. You can push up slightly from behind, and the heart will "pop" up from the border.

9. Tidy and smooth the border from the back and sides with the X-acto knife (Figure 5).

10. Optional: Sprinkle a bit of sparkling embossing powder on the heart (Figure 6).

11. Connect the pin back by embedding the base in a small rectangle of clay; press this on the back of the heart (Figure 7).

12. Bake at 265° for 20 minutes, or as the manufacturer directs. Allow to cool.

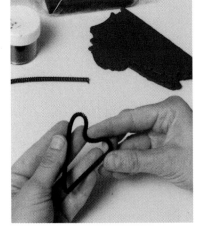

Figure 2

Figure 3

Figure 4

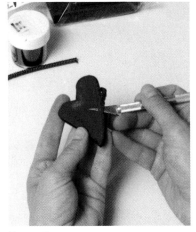

Figure 5

Figure 6

Figure 7

Cocoon Pendant

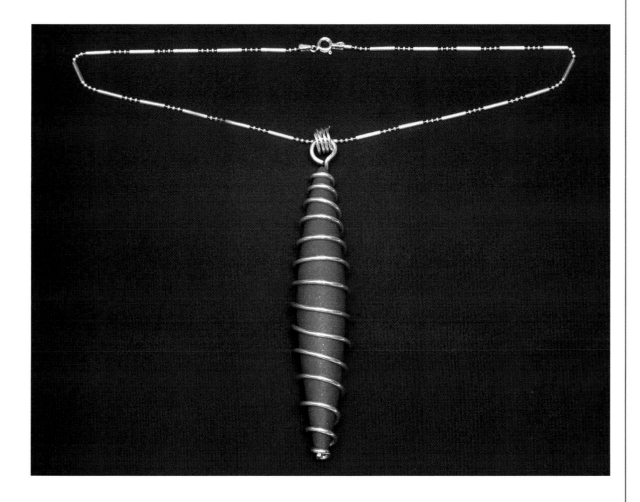

I have always liked the form of a long, fat bead with tapered ends, which resembles a cigar or cocoon. Here, the base is constructed from red sparkle polymer clay which has been baked. This provides a striking contrast to the silver wire. At first, it was my intention to tarnish the silver, but I decided to keep it bright because it complemented the ball and chain link necklace I chose.

■ Materials ■

1-1/2 ft. 14 gauge sterling silver soft wire
FIMO Soft polymer clay, metallic red #202
Round nose pliers
Flush cutters
1/4" mandrel (wood or metal)
Card stock
Oven
Necklace/chain

1. Condition the clay and shape it into a cigar or cocoon form with your palms (Figure 1). Optional: Make several forms in different colors and sizes, if you wish. This gives you options for creating large or small pendants. **Note:** The pendant shown is about 4" long.

2. Bake the clay forms on card stock at 265° for 20 to 30 minutes, or as the manufacturer directs. Allow to cool.

3. Cut 1-1/2 feet of silver wire and begin to twist a small coil using the round nose pliers (Figure 2). Loop the coil a few times, enlarging and expanding the spiral.

4. Insert the bead form into the spiral and adjust the size to fit the pendant by twisting the wire counterclockwise to open the coil. Continue to wrap the form, using pressure to push the wire over the bead (Figure 3).

5. When the coils have tightened and reached the end, make a large eye and bend the loop upright to the form (Figure 4).

6. Wrap several coils around the 1/4" diameter mandrel (Figure 5). Cut with blunt ends.

7. Slide the multiple coils onto the eye of the pendant, as if you were attaching a key chain (Figure 6).

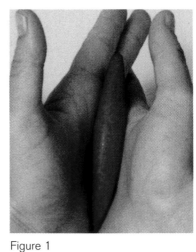

Figure 1

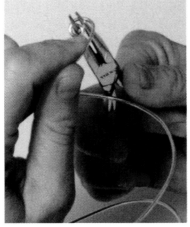

Figure 2

Figure 3

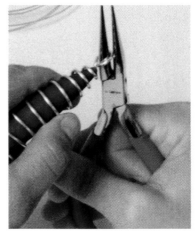

Figure 4

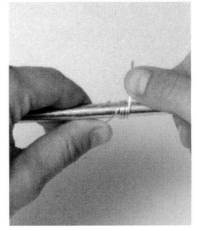

Figure 5

Figure 6

Bali Beads Earrings

The silver beads of Bali are fascinating; here's your chance to use your favorite pair in this classic design. The entire piece is sterling silver, but tarnishing adds natural shading to the silver that is actually an excellent example of value. The coloring, as well as the reflection of light, will make the piece appear more dimensional. The wire wrap adds texture, and the spiral creates a line with movement. You will need to balance the visual weight of the spiral and the top wrap, depending on the size of the bead you choose for this project.

■ Materials ■

1 ft. of 18 gauge sterling soft wire
6" of 20 gauge sterling soft wire
2 ft. of 22 gauge sterling soft wire
Round nose pliers
Flush cutters
Chain nose pliers
Black marker

■ Ear Wires

Note: There are many styles of earring wires, and you can experiment to vary the design.

1. Cut two 3" lengths of 20 gauge wire. Turn an eye pin at one end and bend the wire back from the closure, so the earring will rest away from the closure (Figure 1).

2. Use your thumb as a form to shape the wire and snip at a comfortable length (Figures 2 and 3).

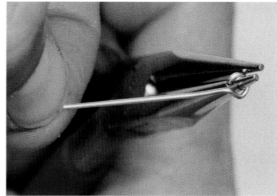

Figure 1

3. File the end smooth so it is not sharp against the skin.

■ Earring

Note: I did this by slipping on a coil I had made in advance with a machine coiler. This is because I have trouble seeing small wire as I wrap it (my vision is in flux). You can also do this design by hand-wrapping the wire and shaping the spiral, but you must be careful not to crush the fine wires as you bend the spiral.

1. Cut two 6" lengths of 18 gauge wire. Measure 4" from the end, mark the silver with the black marker, and make a loose spiral on each piece up to the marked point (Figure 4).

2. Using a small mandrel, coil two 1 ft. lengths of 22 gauge wire. You will have a small piece of wire that looks like a tiny spring. Cut a 3/8" length of coil from each piece to use as the top portion of the design. Now that you have made the components, finish one earring, and then make the other to match (see Step 9).

3. Slip the larger portion of coil over the loose spiral (Figures 5 and 6). Grab the inner circle of the spiral with the round nose pliers, perpendicular to the spiral, to tighten or loosen it. When the desired size is achieved, tighten the inner loop of the 18 gauge wire to secure the coil in place. With chain nose pliers, secure the outer end of the spiral by angling the wire straight up from the spiral (Figure 7).

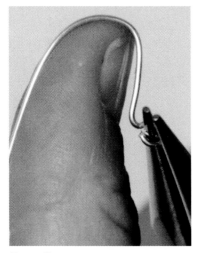
Figure 2

Figure 3

Figure 4

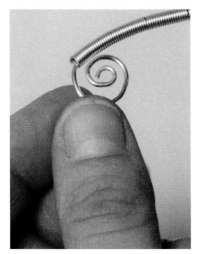
Figure 5

Figure 6

Figure 7

4. Slip on the bead (Figure 8).

5. Slip on the short coil. Adjust the size by clipping away any excess. This may depend on the visual weight of the spiral and the bead.

6. Estimate an amount to close the top with an eye pin loop. This may vary with the loop size you desire. It is acceptable to give yourself extra length and trim the eye as needed. Because eye loops are often used in wire design, you should measure with your finger or something consistent (Figure 9).

7. This spring coil will need to be held firmly as you create the eye (Figure 10). Switching between the chain and round nose pliers will allow you to create angles without marring the wire (Figure 11).

8. Attach the ear wire before closing the eye with the round nose pliers (Figure 12).

9. Repeat Steps 3-8 to create the opposite earring to match (Figure 13).

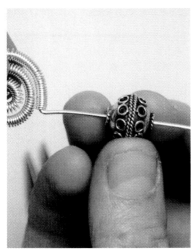

Figure 8

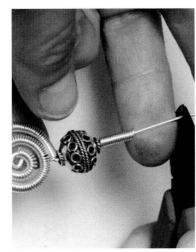

Figure 9

Figure 10

Figure 11

Figure 12

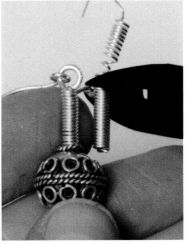

Figure 13

Gold Banded Bracelet

The cords in this bracelet create a lot of lines and movement. The gold is repeated at the center and the catch, as well as in the dangling beads. This is also to move the eye. The gold contrasts with the deep colors of the cords. The cords are gathered so that the wire artwork is at midpoint when the wrist is resting at your side. This creates a curious kind of balance that adds interest in the design and works functionally.

■ Materials ■

16 to 20 strands of cords cut in 2 ft. lengths, colored*
48" gold-filled square half hard wire
Ruler
Marker
Flush cutters
Chain nose pliers
Assorted beads** to dangle from the ends of the
  cords
*The cord used came in one skein of dyed colors.
**Make sure the holes are big enough for the cords.
Note that silver or glass beads will sound like bells,
while polymer clay beads are much quieter!

1. Put all of the cords next to each other; gather them together. Hold them in place with a section of scrap wire (Figure 1).

Figure 1

The project in this photo shows the wrap immediately after making the spiral; however, the instructions double back the wire before the wrap. The two versions create a slightly different line element.

2. Measure and cut 36" of wire; straighten it.

3. Mark 4" from the end of the 36" piece. **Note:** It is important to measure if you want the other end to match.

4. Make a spiral at one end using 4" of wire (Figure 2). Measure the width of the cords and loop the wire back 180° toward itself.

5. Measure the cord again. Using the chain nose pliers, hold the spiral and bend the wire downward to wrap around the cords (Figure 3). Once the wire is bent in this direction, you can place it over the cords and continue bending back and forth to hold the cords in place (Figure 4).

6. When you have 6" left, duplicate the reverse of the top loop from the starting side of the piece and measure another 4" to make the ending spiral (Figure 5). Snip the wire and curl the spiral in the opposing direction.

7. Lay the bracelet over your wrist and gather it with a piece of scrap wire. (I chose to gather it to one side so the beads would dangle at my side rather than under my hand.) Make sure it can slip over the widest portion of your hand.

8. With the remaining 12" piece of wire, make a small spiral at one end, wrap the cords with the wire, and finish the other end of the wire with a reverse spiral (Figures 6 and 7).

9. Thread beads on the ends of the cords and secure with a knot.

Figure 2

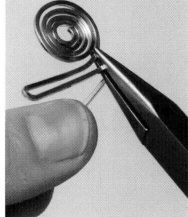
Figure 3

Figure 4

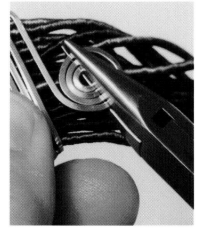
Figure 5

Figure 6

Figure 7

Wire and Clay Bracelet

In this project, wire is utilitarian, but it still is in unity with the design, and you may catch a glimpse of it at any given moment. The plastic coating is complementary to the polymer beads, and the colors add a little contrast to the piece. Form follows function, and the two beads nest together to create a pattern.

■ Materials ■

FIMO Soft polymer clay, red #202 and black metallic sparkle #912
1 ft. each of PVC-coated wire, red, silver, or black
10" elastic cord
1" diameter circle punch
Acrylic brayer or pasta machine
Flush cutters
Large tapestry needle
Small glass or metal spacer beads
Card stock
Oven

1. Condition and flatten the red clay to a 1/16" sheet of clay.

2. Punch several circles in the red clay (Figure 1). There are eleven beads in the bracelet, but you should make a few extra so you can reserve options in the design and size.

3. Cut the wire into 1-1/2" lengths (one for each circle) (Figure 2).

Figure 1

Figure 2

4. Bend the wire in half. Leaving a portion for a loop, twist the wire together once to secure the shape and spread the ends (Figure 3). Twisting and spreading the wire will prevent it from slipping out.

5. Fold the red clay circles over the wire, leaving a portion of wire exposed at the top where the elastic will be threaded (Figure 4). This form resembles a taco shell joined at the top (Figure 5). Smooth the clay at the bend if necessary.

6. Repeat Steps 4 and 5 to make eleven to fifteen beads.

7. Condition and roll a snake of black clay and measure a small portion. This portion should be equal to a 3/8" diameter ball when rolled. Portion the snake into several "beads"

(these will go between the red beads) (Figure 6).

8. Press the clay down on one side with your finger (Figure 7).

9. Poke a hole though the bead at the shallow end with the tapestry needle (Figure 8).

10. Flip the bead and poke the hole through on the opposite side to smooth the hole.

11. Bake all of the beads per the manufacturer's directions (or at 265° for 20 minutes) on the card stock. Allow the beads to cool.

12. String the beads on the elastic cord, alternating the two bead shapes between spacer beads. Knot the elastic ends and cut the excess cord.

Figure 3

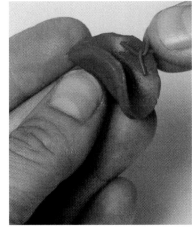
Figure 4

Figure 5

Figure 6

Figure 7

Figure 8

Wire-linked Glass Neckpiece

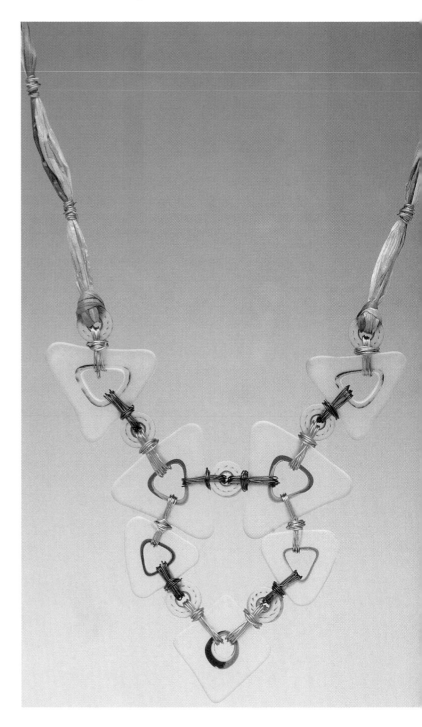

The wire in this design provides a striking contrast to the matte finish of the glass and the cord. The pieces can be arranged in unlimited compositions, but they should all be in the same color family and possess other qualities in common, such as a matte finish, to provide unity in the design. It is also important that you repeat some of the shapes so there is consistency in the design. The centerpiece is in slight contrast with the other components because it is the only square shape; however it is unified in its other characteristics. The small beads at the top of the arrangement creates rhythm and leads the eye to the cords. The cords are also bound with wire to repeat the theme and unify the entire piece. In this design, the emphasis is on the space between the glass beads, as well as the glass beads themselves.

■ Materials ■

6 to 10 pairs of glass shapes with open holes; odd shapes (squares, circles, etc.) can be used for the center pendant
8" of 24 to 26 gauge Artistic Wire in colors that complement the glass beads
Flush cutters
12-foot lengths of raffia cords, colored

Note: To wear the necklace, you can either tie it or attach a latch to the cords with wire.

1. Position the odd shapes to create a pendant (Figure 1). Pair some of the pieces to create balance. Imagine how the linked glass will move and fall with gravity.

2. Cut a length of wire approximately 8". Bend the wire in half and loop it through one of the glass shape's holes where two pieces will be joined.

3. Bend the wire over the glass in the direction of the adjacent bead. Hold the beads slightly apart so there is enough room to wrap the link at midpoint.

4. Thread the wire through the adjacent glass hole, looping both ends several times, connecting the two pieces (Figure 2). Create enough tension so that the link is neat, but leave some space for the wire to go perpendicular to the link in the final wrap. When then glass is sufficiently connected, usually five wraps, cross the remaining wire over each other at the midpoint and continue to wrap the wire around the midsection, perpendicular to the first wrap. When the midsection is sufficiently wrapped, turn the pieces to the backside and twist the two wire ends together. Tucked the ends underneath the wrapped wires and snip the excess wire.

5. Proceed to the next bead and begin to build the entire chain of glass beads, held together by the wrapped links.

6. Cut two 3-foot lengths of raffia cord for each side of the necklace. Gather two cords and fold in half. Thread the bent end through a glass bead (Figure 3). Poke the cord ends through the loop and tighten (Figure 4).

7. Wrap the cords with the wire at even intervals (Figure 5). Attach a small bead to the end of the cord.

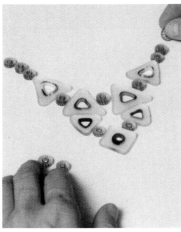

Figure 1

Figure 2

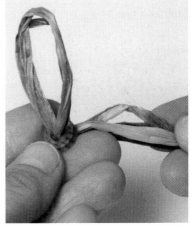

Figure 3

Figure 4

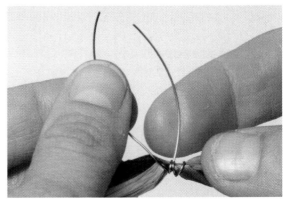

Figure 5

Paper Cone Sculpture

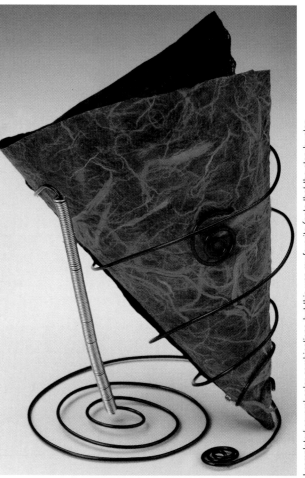

I completed several color combinations, but this was my favorite (note that the step-by-step photographs show brass wire rather than blue for the base).

*W*ire can create a form in seconds. In this project, I used another immediate material, paper. The two materials provide an interesting contrast as well as a texture contrast (the smooth wire and the crinkled paper). The colors are from an intense, rich palette. The piece is balanced, literally as well as visually. The repetition of the spiral unifies the design.

■ Materials ■

3 to 4 ft. of 14 gauge brass wire
3 ft. of 18 gauge craft wire, your choice of contrasting color
Mandrel or twist machine to wrap a 6" to 8" spring
Heavy handmade mulberry paper, your choice of color
Scissors, compass, pencil
Flush cutters
Needle nose pliers

1. The base is free-formed with spirals. First, create a spiral base all on the same plane, beginning with a large spiral and working inward. The tighter the spiral the more it is hardened, so this is advantageous as you approach the middle and strengthen the piece at the same time. You may have to "spring" the coil in and out to counter-balance the tension so it remains flat.

2. Bend the wire upright and straighten an 8" length (Figure 1).

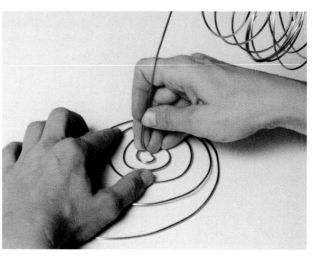

Figure 1

3. Estimate the size of the second spiral (the carrier) that will hold the paper cup and snip the length. Create a freehand spiral that diminishes in size (Figure 2).

4. Cut a three-quarter circle (the diameter shown was 10") from the mulberry paper. Overlap the edges to make a cone. Fit to the width of the carrier spiral (Figure 3).

5. The cone is connected with a paper clip made of wire. Cut a 15" length and make a large, flat spiral. Begin with pliers, but complete the spiral by hand. Leave about 4" at the end.

6. Poke the end through the paper (Figure 4). Carefully twist another freehand spiral on the inside of the cup. Press the inside clip-spiral against the outside clip-spiral to tighten the grasp the clip is providing.

7. Make another clip to insert on the other side of the cone, so that the weight of the clay doesn't pull the cone to one side. Set the cone aside.

8. Create a large coil of wire 6" to 8" as needed for the height of the sculpture. Slip this through the cone holder and onto the straight portion of the wire (Figure 5). Don't worry if it balances yet; you will finish and adjust it after you insert the cone.

9. Once the wire coil is slid over the wire, adjust the carrier loop as the spiral diminishes to bring the spiral to a tightened close at the foot of where the cone will rest.

10. Insert the cone and bend all of the wires to balance.

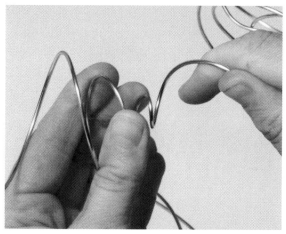

Figure 2

Figure 3

Figure 4

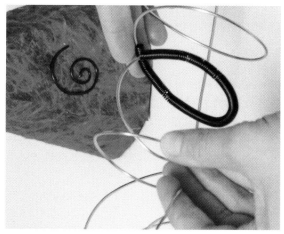

Figure 5

Wire Spine Book

ere, wire has a functional purpose, as well as decorative. The contrast with the polymer clay is striking but has enough relation to the gold embedded in the cover design. The coiled buttons also repeat the use of the wire, giving the piece unity. The copper wire is complementary to the earth tones, and it will tarnish over time, giving the piece more value (light to dark). Antiquing the clay panels also creates value.

■ Materials ■

FIMO Soft polymer clay, earth tones (brown, orange, or ochre)
Magic Leaf gold leaf
African design stamp (that shown is from Limited Editions Rubberstamps)
Oven
Card stock
Roller
Blade
Scissors
Round nose pliers
Chain nose pliers
Flush cutters
Hand drill tool
Fine manicure sanding sponge
Cloth rag
Acrylic paint, in burnt sienna
Popsicle stick
Mulberry paper, orange
Bone folder
3 ft. of 18 gauge copper wire
Crafter's Pick Ultimate Tacky Glue
Super glue
Optional: Polymer clay varnish

1. Condition the polymer clay and cut two flat panels about 1/8" thick for the book cover, either 3" x 4" or 3" x 3".

2. Place a sheet of gold leaf over both pieces of the clay and press the stamp into the sur-

face. The leaf will act as a release, preventing the stamp from sticking (Figure 1). Stamp both the front and back panels

3. Bake the panels as the clay manufacturer directs (or at 265° for 20 minutes) on the card stock. Allow to cool.

4. Using the fine manicure sponge, sand the surface of the panels. Where the design is impressed, the gold leaf will remain intact.

Figure 1

5. Lightly cover the panels with a thin coat of burnt sienna acrylic paint. Remove any excess with the rag; the piece should look antiqued (Figure 2). The paint will act as a protective covering to the gold, but you may also choose to apply an additional coat of varnish made for polymer clay.

6. Cut a strip of mulberry paper the height of the book panels and 24" long. A larger number of pages may make the book thicker than the spine. Fold the paper into an accordion, using the panel as a measurement. Burnish the folds with the bone folder.

7. Glue the two end panels of the accordion paper to the inside of the book covers with Crafter's Pick glue. Smooth with the bone folder.

8. Pull the pages aside and drill two holes in the corners of the cover panels where you will attach the wire lever to the spine (Figure 3). The holes in the front cover will be to the left of the design; the holes in the back cover will be to the right.

9. To make the copper spine, cut 1-1/2 feet of copper wire and wrap it loosely (so it will release) around the Popsicle stick. Remove it from the stick and cut it to the size of the spine, the length of the distance between the two holes in the cover.

10. Make four spirals to serve as buttons for the holes, front and back (Figure 4). Each spiral should take about 4" of wire. Place these buttons over the holes on the front and back and secure with super glue.

11. Place an 8" length of wire centered through the spine and then angle both ends toward the book cover. Bend the wire down over each hole and push the ends through the buttons and the book cover (Figures 5, 6, and 7). The book needs to be open to accomplish this. Once the wires are poked through, you can wind them in a spiral on the inside and tighten them to secure the spine to the book (Figure 8).

12. Secure the back to the spine in the same way.

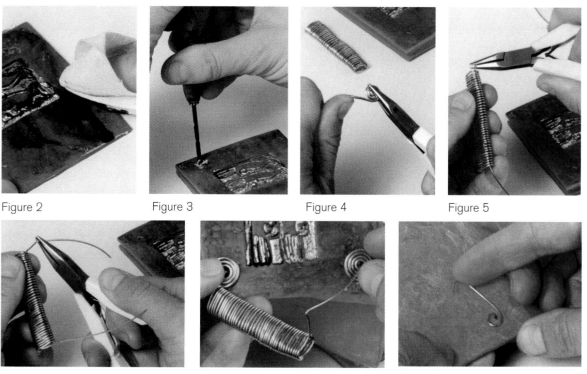

Figure 2   Figure 3   Figure 4   Figure 5

Figure 6   Figure 7   Figure 8

Contour Wire Drawing

*W*ire is a line, and this case, it is literally a line drawing. The broken wire (line) indicates a shift in the plane of the drawn subject's form. This is how depth is indicated in a line drawing. A line that is in front of another line indicates that the form is at a closer distance than its surroundings. Another aspect of the quality of space is that large open areas allow the simple lines to be very effective. Any additional decoration would be too competitive and detract from the emphasis of the suggested figure.

■ Materials ■

5" x 7" piece of glass
Picture of figure
Tracing paper and pencil
Whack-It-Down
FIMO Classic polymer clay Black #9
Pasta machine or acrylic brayer
Flush cutters
Approximately 6" of 22 gauge gold-filled wire
FIMO Varnish
Card stock
Oven
Frame with tabs

1. With the pencil and tracing paper, trace a figure drawing of a model from a magazine or photograph. Use only enough lines to illustrate the form. Make several drawings and choose one that is your favorite (Figure 1).

Figure 1

2. Position the glass over the drawing and pencil along the edge of the glass to frame the composition. Cut and bend each piece of wire by hand to match the shape of the lines, clipping the ends (Figure 2).

3. Whack each piece down with the Whack-It-Down to harden and flatten the wire (Figure 3).

4. Condition the black polymer clay and create a 1/16" sheet of clay. Cover the glass with the polymer clay. Place the original drawing over the black clay so it fits in the drawing. Gently impress the traced image into the clay with the pencil; this impression indicates where the wire pieces will be placed (Figure 4).

5. Remove the paper and position the wire pieces into place. Press them gently into the clay (Figure 5).

6. Bake the entire piece (including glass) on a sheet of card stock at 265° for 20 minutes or as the manufacturer directs. Allow it to completely cool.

7. Cover the piece with varnish to protect the clay and the wire.

8. Frame the piece.

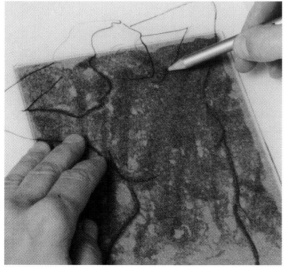
Figure 2

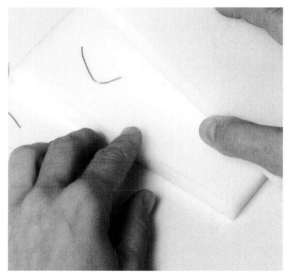
Figure 3

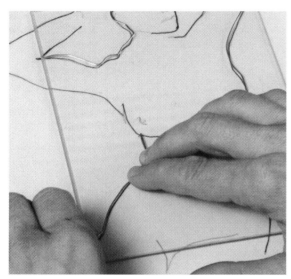
Figure 4

Figure 5

Serving Tray

ustav Klimt, the incredible Austrian painter, inspired this tray. You may not see the connection, but similar patterns and shapes are what I had in mind when I started. As I was creating the design, I settled for a much less complicated piece. I also liked the large amount of space. A single wire line creates a rhythmic pattern. The little beads also added variety to the pattern—both with color and spacing, but they repeat the circles in the red wire. I tried many variations of the composition, and even added more lines, but the design with the most space was the most appealing. Also in consideration of spatial relations, notice how the wire on top of the mesh has more spatial depth in the arrangement than the red wire and beads. There are no straight lines in the composition. The organic flowing lines create a unity between the different materials.

■ Materials ■

Creative Paperclay* or air drying paper clay

Plastic wrap (if the project is not completed in one sitting)

18" to 24" of 22 gauge Artistic Wire colored copper wire, maroon and forest green

12 ft. of 22 gauge Artistic Wire colored copper wire, gun metal

Coiling Gizmo or mandrel for creating coiled edges

Small glass beads, purple/brown matte finish

2" x 8" strip of fine brass wire mesh (or paper, cloth, or metal strip)

Flush cutters

Scissors

Roller or acrylic brayer

Serving tray**

EnviroTex Light acrylic surface sealant

Wig Jig

Whack-It-Down or hammer

* I chose this product because it could be painted and was compatible to the sealant.

**The tray shown is 5" x 8", but you can use any size.

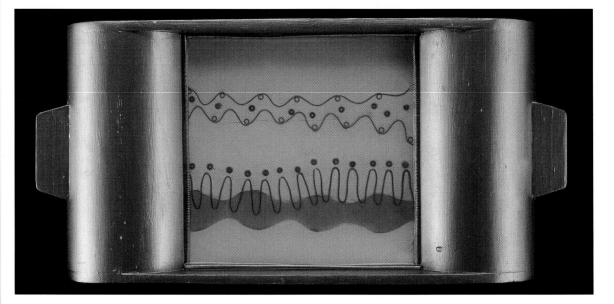

Wire *in* Design

1. Used a jig to create a pattern in the wire. Lift the wire from the jig, shift and replace the strand on the jig, and continue the pattern to create a length long enough reach both ends of the tray (Figure 1).

2. Make several lengths and patterns to consider while creating the composition. Straighten and harden the wire by whacking or hammering it to even the surface plane (Figure 2).

3. Cut the mesh or paper with a wavy line to fit the length of the tray (Figure 3).

4. Cover the tray floor evenly with the paper-clay (Figure 4). The clay should be about 1/8" thick. **Note:** If you need to pause, cover the clay with plastic wrap.

5. Arrange the lines, beads, and mesh on the tray surface as shown, or in your own unique composition (Figure 5 and 6). Once the design is worked out, press the pieces into the surface of the clay. This is a little challenging, and you may have to re-even the surface plane of the wire. Sometimes, the clay will actually help to hold the wire down. Smooth the surface with your finger or plastic wrap stretched over your finger.

6. Allow the piece to dry (this may take a day or so); it may shrink a little and need refilling at the edges or in any gaps.

7. Make coils to go into the borders to cover any shrinkage and finish the edges.

8. Prepare the EnviroTex Light sealant, per the manufacturer's directions, and drop the coils into the edges. Apply the sealant and allow the tray to cure in a ventilated area.

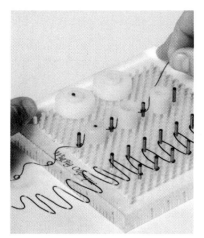
Figure 1

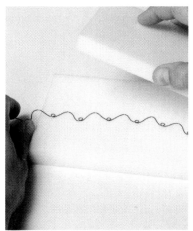
Figure 2

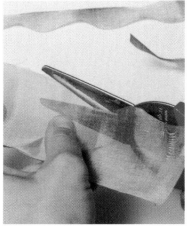
Figure 3

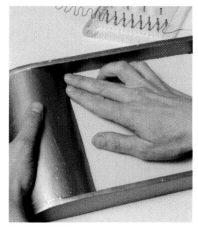
Figure 4

Figure 5

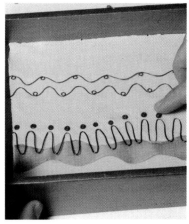
Figure 6

Projects

The Trivet

One day, I was strolling through an antique shop, and I saw a really cool trivet made out of old wire—but it was $65. The lines were in a perfect spiral, radiating out from the middle. It was sewn together with thinner gauge wire, and I felt confident I could grasp the concept.

I had a resolve to use tie wire, the black, heavy tie wire from the hardware store, because I desired that "iron hearth" look.

I started by making a cross with looped ends. Ah—good time to learn to twist. Not exactly the twist as in rock 'n roll, but by the time I had twisted this wire, I felt really out of shape. I found out that it is better to hold on to something, such as pliers, and then twist. And then it is actually more effective to twist the pliers rather than the wire. So I twisted my four looped ends and cut extra lengths at the middle. At this time,

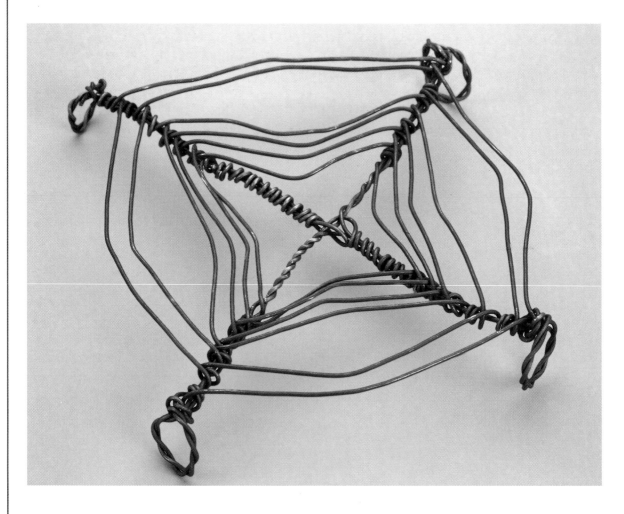

I learned the twist and snap method of cutting. Previously, I had only experienced score, bend, and snap, but the idea of putting my beautiful jewelry pliers into that cold hard steel made me wiggle and squirm. My squirming ended up to be an efficient way of snapping the wire. It also served as a foreboding clue that if I twisted this stuff *too* much I would have to start over. No way. By this time, my hands were pitch black. The phone was now contaminated, too. I wondered if wire artists ever used gloves. I also wondered if I would ever use this 5 lb. spool of wire again. No wonder they use wire to keep people out of places—you are marked for life.

My project, however, had hope. I decided to go forth with something resembling the "eye of God," a toy I had been deprived of making in my childhood. I wrapped the long ends at the middle of the cross and extended the wrapping outward opposite the midpoint. I then twisted the other two cross sections. This work extended about 2" from the middle, and I felt my cross was secure. (I also remembered my model had 6 spokes.) I decided to be inventive.

I looked at the spool and thought no way am I carrying that thing in and out of spokes, I will just have to guess. So I guessed at how many loops (conveniently it was already looped) and then decided I had enough. I did not want to turn this into a math project—math is not art to me, and I wanted the excitement of the risk.

I proceeded to wrap the wire, connecting the spokes, first securing the wire at a starting point (the inside of the wrapped spoke) and then wrapping two times around each extending arm. It is advantageous to continue in the same direction. At times, I had to count and compare how many strands had been completed—and then continue in the direction that was short of connections.

There are two ways to wrap: you can wrap the wire around the project, or you can wrap the project around the wire. I found I got the best results wrapping the project around the wire. This meant that the trivet was upside down at moments and it got a little confusing. I had this preponderance about over and under but somehow going in a constant direction; it just seemed to work out by itself.

I looped the ends of the twists into a circle because they were longer than I needed. Then I twisted, snapped, and tucked the ends where they wouldn't scratch anything. I bent the circles perpendicular to the woven wire plate and Voila—my project looked like a 5-year-old made it. Now here's where I can really illustrate the value of design even if options are limited. I decided to bend the connecting wires in their middles, either in or out with a decided "crook." This made everything point in or out and put an interesting gap between the lines. Thus, by adding space and movement, my trivet became a masterpiece—it's definitely one of a kind!

Simple Silver Link

This little link can be an accent to a pendant, a link in a chain, or a pair of earrings. It is a good project to practice basic wire skills (see pages 24 to 28).

■ Materials ■

12" 18 gauge sterling wire for each link
6" 16 gauge sterling wire for eye pin (3" used, 6" to aid grasp)
Round nose pliers
Chain nose pliers
Flush cutters

1. Snip the 12" 18 gauge wire so that both ends are flush cut. Bend it in half over the 6" 16 gauge wire, which will serve as a mandrel, the core of the link, and the eye pin. Wrap until you can measure 4" from the end (Figure 1).

2. Turn the piece around to work on the opposite end. Unwrap a coil at midpoint and begin to wrap again (this makes the wrap more uniform). Wrap until you can measure 4" at the end. Using the round nose pliers, make a spiral turning inward toward the wrap (Figure 2).

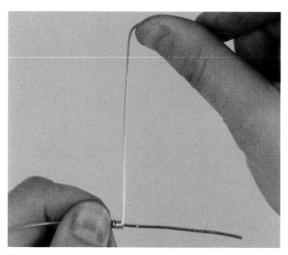

Figure 1

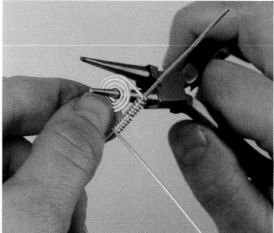

Figure 2

3. Measure the placement on the nose of the pliers and begin the opposite spiral in the same place on the pliers. This way, the two spirals will match in size of the inner circle.

4. Snip the ends of the core wire in a flush cut. Make an eye pin on both ends of the wrap (Figure 3). You will have wire left over, but you can use it for another link. (I prefer to begin with a longer piece and keep cutting it as each link is made.)

5. Twist the spirals away from the wrap and then angle alongside the wrap using the chain nose pliers (Figures 4 and 5).

6. Add dangling parts with jump rings (Figure 6).

7. See Project 7 for earring hooks.

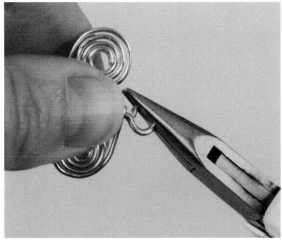

Figure 3

Figure 4

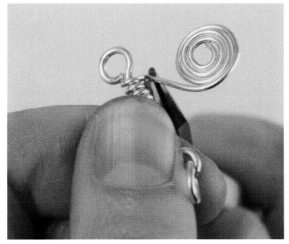

Figure 5

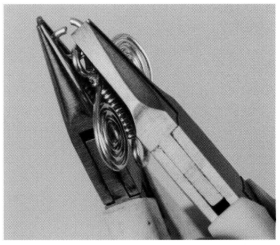

Figure 6

CONTRIBUTING ARTISTS

Edward Ackfeld
Ackfeld Mfg.
P.O. Box 539
Reeds Spring, MO 65737
888-272-3135
ackfeldwire@tri-lakes.net
www.ackfeldwire.com

Kat Allison
Copperleaf Designs
757-875-5156
cpprlf@aol.com
http://members.aol.com/cpprlf/
copperleaf.html

Cathy Ames
Treasures
280 Jackson Creek Dr.
Jacksonville, OR 97530
541-899-0292

Deborah Anderson
A Thousand Canes
265 N. 13th St.
San Jose, CA 95112
408-998-5303
maraha@aol.com

Merideth Arnold
Moonstars Unltd.
110 N. 201 St.
Shoreline, WA 98133-3012
marnold@nwlink.com
www.photopoint.com

Shana Astrachan
1777 Yosemite Ave. #350
San Francisco, CA 94124
415-822-7736
sastra@earthlink.net
www.shanaastrachan.com

Laura Balombini
P.O. Box 733
Blue Hill, ME 04614
207-374-5142
lbalombini@media2.hypernet.
com
www.balombini.com

Nancy Banks
627 Orvis
San Jose, CA 95112
408-279-5144
banks@gobanks.com
www.gobanks.com

MJ Bennett
MJ Bennett Designs
415-454-0188
escapade1@home.com

Susie Bingham
6418 Berwickshire Way
San Jose, CA 95120
408-268-4718
smrb@ziplink.net

Jerome Bourcy
B.J.'s Creative Wirework
11434 Eucalyptus Hills Dr.
Lakeside, CA 92040
619-561-2561
bjswire@abac.com
www.bjswire.com

Rhonda Buckels
Eclectic Expressions
www.gr8jewelry4u.com

Mike Buesseler

Bob Calton
300 Broadway St. #208
St. Paul, MN 55101
651-222-2287
bobcalton@aol.com
www.bobcalton.com

Mark Case, Sr.
Wire Art Jewelry
657 Woodmen Camp Trail
Randleman, NC 27317
336-495-2478
markcase@aol.com
www.markcase.com

Maj-Britt Cawthon
11715 18th Ave.
Lakewood, CO 80215
303-274-7565

Rene J. Cigler
Cigler Designs
5875 Doyle St. #10
Emeryville, CA 94608
510-594-0844
rcigler@inkmonster.com
www.renecigler.com

Jean Comport
macduff@voyager.net

Diane Cook
17757 Killany Dr.
Holt, MI 48842
wdpstudio@dellnet.com

Loren Damewood
Golden Knots
P.O. Box 48543
St. Petersburg, FL 33743
727-347-0593
lorenzo@goldenknots.com
www.golden-knots.com

Cynthia Darling
Darling Creations
P.O. Box 225058
415-759-9691
simplydarling@yahoo.com

Linda Darrell-Lockhart
WireArt Jewelry
Gilden Script
P.O. Box 511
Tomball, TX 77377
281-357-5060
linda@gildenscript.com
www.gildenscript.com

Tina Deweese
Down to the Wire
14190 Cottonwood Canyon
Bozeman, MT 59718
406-763-4221
tina@deweeseart.com
www.deweeseart.com

Celie Fago
Handmade
RR 1 376
Bethel VT 05032
802-234-5428
vfago@aol.com

Susan Marie Freda
Angel Marie Studios
1034 Virginia St. Apt B
Berkeley, CA 94810
845-339-4919
angelmarie12@hotmail.com

Denise Gaffney
Dema Designs
P.O. Box 577467
Modesto, CA 95357
209-985-5033
denise@asthewebspins.com
www.asthewebspins.com/dema

Vlad Gavrilyuk
Student artist
Gwen Gibson
216 Bayview St.
San Rafael, CA 94901
415-454-3246
www.gwengibson.com

Chris Gluck
15 Poker Hill Rd.
Underhill, VT 05489
802-899-3659
cgluck@together.net

Linda Goff
Quirkworks
1204 Fir St.
Olympia, WA 98501
360-352-4701

LeRoy Goertz
The Refiner's Fire
P.O. Box 66612
Portland, OR 97290
503-775-5242
lgoertz@qwest.net
www.coilinggizmo.com

Corrine Gurry
The Wire Wizard
P.O. Box 50312
Bellevue, WA 98015
425-644-1009
beadlady@wolfenet.com
www.thewirewizard.com

P.K. Hille-Hatten
jonandkay@home.com

B.J. Hites
1388 Haight St. Box 136
San Francisco, CA 94117
415-647-5811
bghites@hotmail.com

Julianna C. Hudgins
Julianna Productions
856-374-1234
juliannahudgins@aol.com
www.thecreativecornerwith
julianan.com

Diane Hyde
Diane H. Designs
P.O. Box 1433
Brookfield, WI 53008
262-574-1324
dianehdesigns@execpe.com

Amy Jin Yu Kuang
Student artist

Dianne Karg
www.wrapturewirejewelry.ou.ca

Donna Kato
Prarie Craft
P.O. Box 209
Florissant, CO 80816
www.prairiecraft.com

Kim Korringa
156 Eldorado Dr.
Mountainview, CA 94041
650-969-1790
kimcreates@aol.com

Margaret Kristof
P.O. Box 752
Pinole, CA 94564
510-741-8578

Debbie Krueger
27426 Hufsmith Rd.
Magnolia, TX 77354
281-356-8541
dbriank@aol.com

Claudia Lam-Siem
Student artist

Karen Lechner
Link by Link
Box 47047 300 Borough Dr.
Toronto, Ontario MIP427
Canada
416-289-4765
karen.lechner@home.com

Anna Lemons
937-833-6142
metroanna@aol.com

Desiree McCrorey
ddmcc@yahoo.com

Barbara A. McGuire
Design Innovations
P.O. Box 472334
San Francisco, CA 94147
415-922-6366
bmcguire@claystamp.com
www.claystamp.com

Dottie McMillan
7060 Fire Side Dr.
Riverside, CA 92506
909-780-4052
dmcmillan@earthlink.net
www.kaleidoscopes4u.com

Lynne Merchant
P.O. Box 230594
Encinitas, CA 92023

Marilyn Milam
281-568-2523
www.milams.com/wired

Ava Minski Foxman
Moonbabies
888-MOONBABY
moonbabies@aol.com

Anne and Karen Mitchell
AnKara Designs
2323 Pinecrest Dr.
Altadena, CA 91001
626-798-8491
www.ankaradesigns.com

Beverly Morgan
BAM Designs
2063 S. Edgewater
Mesa, AZ 85208
bamorgan035@aol.com

Pat Moses-Caudel
P.O. Box 5111
Richmond, CA 94805
510-724-4867
wildpoppy1@aol.com

Lynda Musante
Nifty Development Corp.
804-463-6409

Randy Neu
Whimsical Wire
631 James Ct.
West Bend, WI 53095
262-338-8414
randy@whimsicalwire.com
www.bubblewands.com

Patricia Newton
Patricia's Designs
925-736-4434

Kathy Peterson
Kathy Peterson Products, Inc.
18709 S.E. River Ridge Rd.
Tequesta, FL 33469
561-744-2086
651-744-9199 fax
kp@kathypeterson.com
www.kathypeterson.com

Vaneka Reed
Student artist

Steven Reinhold

Preston Reuther
Master Wire Sculptor
www.wire-sculpture.com

Nan Robkin
P.O. Box 70024
Bellevue, WA 98005
alhrobkin@aol.com

Timothy Rose
Bldg. 153 4th & Waterfront
Mare Island, Vallejo, CA 94592
707-562-3158
troseart@aol.com
www.mobilesculpture.com

Steve Rova
10094 6th St Ste. A
Rancho Cucamonga, CA 91730
909-553-4052
rovacat@hotmail.com

Jan Sage
jsage@hewm.com

Veena Santhigoset
Distinctive Designs
415-647-2131

Marvin and Michelle Shafer
Q3 Art, Inc.
1056 W. Wellington
Chicago, IL 60657
773-525-3729
www.q3art.com

Rosana Shushtar
Student artist

Gail Siegel
A GHS Designs
1275 Noe St.
San Francisco, CA 94114
415-647-0489
gsiegel@fm-ucsf.edu

Barbara Becker Simon
5232 SW 11th Place
Cape Coral, FL 33914
941-549-5971
midas@iline.com
www.bbsimon.com

Alison Bailey Smith
San Francisco, CA
abs1000@hotmail.com

Jim Stone
P.O. Box 4763
Boulder, CO 80306
jamesjstone@hotmail.com

David Strongheart
Dancing Bubbles
4500 E Speedway Blvd. Ste. 41
Tucson, AZ 85712
520-721-6318
www.dancingbubbles.com

Mike Talgoy
Wireworks Puzzles
mtalgoy@escape.ca
www.wireworkspuzzles.com

Ann Turpin Thayer
Tapestries of Light
480-598-9090
tapestries-of-light@home.com
www.tapestriesoflight.com

Lisa Toland
545 Bloomfield Road
Sebastopol, CA 95472
707-823-6890
707-823-7266 fax

Pier Voulkos
1250 57th Ave. #24
Oakland, CA 94621
510-533-8112
Pier4Dan@aol.com

Rob Weilgoszinski
1651 Market #302
San Francisco, CA 94103
415-861-1978
wyzzard5@aol.com
www.stromloader.com/wyzzard

Ellen Wieski
cafew@hypernet.com

Razine M. Wenneker
Ellie Rose Link-Able Designs,
L.L.C.
P.O. Box 37003
St. Louis, MO 63141
link-able@ix.netcom.com
www.link-able.bigstep.com

Wendy Witchner
707-937-3804

Sherie Yazman
sfteachart@aol.com

Jill York O'Bright
Joy Jewelry
526 E. Monroe Ave.
St. Louis, MO 63122
314-822-9847
obright@i1.net

SUPPLY SOURCES

Accent Import - Export, Inc.
P.O. Box 4361
Walnut Creek, CA 94596
800-989-2889
www.fimozone.com
FIMO polymer clay, Fun Wire (poly-coated), modeling tools.

American Art Clay Co.
4717 16th St.
Indianapolis, IN 46222
800-374-1600
www.amaco.com
FIMO polymer clay, Funwire (poly-coated), modeling tools.

Art Mecca
300 Brannan Street, Ste. 503
San Francisco, CA 94107
800-414-4230
www.artmeca.com
Artist website, art for sale.

Artistic Wire
P.O. Box 1347
Elmhurst, IL 60126
630-530-7567
www.artisticwire.com
Colored copper wires gauges 18-26, metallic, opaque, and poly-coated finishes.

Beadalon
205 Carter Drive
West Chester PA 19382
800-824-WIRE (9473)
www.beadalon.com
Colored copper wire, jewelry stringing wire.

Beadbox
800-BEADBOX
Mail order beads, findings, wire, anodized aluminum wire, tools, jigs.

CGM Supply
Wholesale silver and gold wire and findings.

David H. Fell & Company, Inc.
P.O. Box 910952
Los Angeles, CA 90091
800-822-1996
www.dhfco.com
Fine metals and wires, patterned metal sheets.

Design Originals
2425 Cullen St.
Fort Worth, TX 76107
800-877-7820
www.d-originals.com
Craft how-to books.
Wire Baskets #5079, by Mary Harrison.
Wire Décor #3291, by Kathy Peterson.
Wire Jewelry #3292, by Linda Muscante.
Coiled Wire Jewelry #03299, by LeRoy Goertz.

Indian Jewelers Supply Co.
601 East Coal Avenue
Gallop, NM 87301
800-545-6540
www.ijsinc.com
Fine metal wires, findings, beads, cabochons.

Master Wire Sculptor Videos
www.wire-sculpture.com
Wire sculpting wire videos, home business plans.

Metaliferous
34 West 46th St.
New York, NY 10036
212-944-0909
www.metaliferous.com
Fine metal wires, findings, Precious Metal Clay.

Praixair
1690 Evans Ave.
San Francisco, CA 94102
415-826-8627
Welding supplies, metal rods.

The Refiners Fire
P.O. Box 66612
Portland, OR 97290
503-775-5242
www.coilinggizmo.com
The Coiling Gizmo (all models), videos, books.

Rio Grande
6901 Washington NE
Albuquerque, NM 87109
800-545-6566

The Shepherdess
2802 Juan St #18
San Diego, CA 92110
619-297-4110
Bead store with classes featuring guest artists, wire tools, sterling wire.

Soft Flex
P.O. Box 80
Sonoma, CA 95476
707-938-3539
www.softflexcompany.com
Complete range of tools, wire, books, videos, jigs, Twist 'n' Curl wrapping tool.

Thunderbird Supply Company
1907 W. Historic Route 66
Gallup, NM 87301
505-722-4323
www.tbscorp.com
Sterling wire, jewelry findings, beads.

Wig Jig, Helwig Industries
PO Box 5306
Arlington, VA 22205
8000-579-WIRE
www.wigjig.com
Acrylic wire jig.

Wire Art, Duncan Enterprises
5673 East Shields Ave.
Fresno, CA 93727
800-438-6226
www.wirearts.com
www.duncancrats.com
Wire kits, poly-coated wire.

The Wire Artist
P.O. Box 21105
Strattford, Ont.
Canada N5A7V4
519-461-1902
www.mag.on.ca
Magazine for wire artists.

Wire Wizard
P.O. Box 50312
Bellevue, WA 98015
888-547-4447
www.thewirewizard.com
Wire, tools, Wire Wizard jigs, videos.

BIBLIOGRAPHY

Baal-Teshuva, Jacob. *Alexander Calder*. Benedikt Taschen Verlag GmbH. 1998.

Ball, Michael. *Wire Magic: 2000*. Cincinnati OH: North Light Books, F&W Publications. 2000.

Baskett, Mickey. *Wire Works: An Easy Decorative Craft*. New York: Sterling Publishing Co. 1999.

Clegg, Helen and Mary Larom. *Making Wire Jewelry*. Ashvillle, NC: Lark Books. 1997.

Cusick, Dawn. *Making Bead & Wire Jewelry*. New York: Lark Books, Sterling Publishing Co. Inc. 2000.

Fisch, Arline M. *Textile Techniques in Metal*. Ashville, NC: Lark Books. 1996.

Lareau, Mark. *All Wired Up*. Interweave Press. 2000.

Lidstone, John. *Building With Wire*. New York: Van Nostrand Reinhold. 1972.

Lipman, Jean. *Calder's Universe*. New York: The Viking Press. 1976.

Maguire, Mary. *Wirework*. London: Lorenz Books, Anness Publishing Co. 1996.

Marchesseau, Daniel. *The Intimate World of Alexander Calder*. Paris. 1989.

McNiff, Shaun. *Trust the Process: An Artist's Guide to Letting Go*. Boston: Shambala Publications, Inc. 1998.

McSwiney, Sharon, Penny Williams, Claire C. Davies, and Jennie Davies. *The Creative Jeweler*. Iola, WI: Krause Publications. 2000.

Slesin, Suzanne, Daniel Rozensztroch, Jean Louis Menard, Stafford Cliff, and Gilles deChabaneix. *Everyday Things Wire*. New York: Abbeville Publishing Co. 1994.

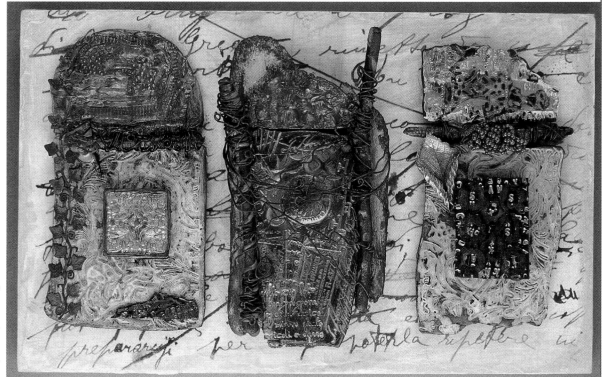

Tres portes by Jann Sage.

INDEX